New Packaging Design

New Packaging Design

Janice Kirkpatrick/ Graven Images

Laurence King Publishing

LAURENCE KING

For Jean, who believes that anything is possible, and Ross, who expects the impossible.

Published in 2009 by
Laurence King Publishing Ltd
361–373 City Road
London EC1V 1LR
Tel +44 20 7841 6900
Fax +44 20 7841 6910
E-mail enquiries@
laurenceking.com
www.laurenceking.com

Frontispiece: Vine Parma, by
Raya Ivanovskaya, Russia, 2008.
These ethnic-inspired wine
labels are distinctively different.

A catalogue record for this book is
available from the British Library.

ISBN 978 1 85669 613 5

Designed by GraphicalHouse
Research by Emma Murphy

Printed in China

Contents

Intro

Packaging may have been around for thousands of years but it has only now come of age. Today it is big business, big news and a big part of our lives. This zeitgeist is exemplified by Zhang Yin, China's richest woman, who in just over a decade has amassed a $3.4 billion (£2.8 billion) fortune through her Nine Dragons Paper Industries Company that recovers waste paper from the United States and recycles it as high-quality paperboard in a packaging conveyor belt that spans the world. The eye of this global tornado is pressured by issues ranging from sustainability, technology, the revolution in agriculture, globalization, climate change and industrialization, to the growth in materialism, hypermarkets, competition and the migration of populations. Overlay this with the West's rich mercantile heritage, and the evolution of the design industries, and there are some pretty amazing packs with fabulous stories to tell.

Many packs express local cultures and traditions in order to appear distinctive and attractive in the global marketplace while others exploit psychology and physiology to intuitively communicate how they should be used. Some packages are dressed up as precious gifts to emphasize their financial or personal value and their social currency – there are even packs that must be destroyed before they yield their contents.

While many people consider packaging to be a byword for 'waste', its value is actually beyond money and materials. To reduce it to mere 'packaging' is a common mistake because it ignores its complexity and the vital role packs play in making products competitive and our lives vibrant and interesting. Furthermore, climate change has compelled the manufacturers and designers of packaging to become more environmentally aware. Consequentially many packs are increasingly constructed energy-efficiently using recycled, recyclable, biodegradable and sustainable materials in their production.

Just so we are clear from the outset – I am a designer and I am especially interested in how and why packs have evolved, how they look and perform, how they're made, what they are made of, and what they mean culturally and economically. I like to figure out what we buy and why. When it comes to packaging design we are all unconscious experts. I am amazed by how much we use our intuition when we decide what to buy and keep, and what to throw away. I do not believe in the concept of impulse purchases because each impulse is composed of many sub-conscious decisions. One of the purposes of this book is to reveal how packaging functions simultaneously at many different levels in order to influence what we decide to buy.

From the start I knew there was no way I could write a comprehensive book about packaging design because it would be an impossible task. Instead I used my experience – as a travelled, professional designer – to select the packs that attracted me, that I thought twice about, that intrigued me, that were new, different or exciting, or that had hidden dimensions. I also experimented. Sometimes I shopped like a customer, while on other occasions I changed my perspective and shopped from the viewpoint of an environmentalist, a food manufacturer, a printer, a retailer or even a conceptual artist. Sometimes I simply shopped. The biggest surprises came when I comfort-shopped on autopilot and found products that reminded me of my childhood, evoking a less complicated mercantile past untrammelled by disclaimers, marketing science or sophisticated production techniques. Sometimes simplicity and sincerity are best. After all, the most modest packs often have the greatest and strangest stories to tell.

To help understand the many different ways in which packaging functions, this book is divided into four sections: packs that protect, preserve, perform or promote. Because most packs do all four things simultaneously the divisions are necessarily broad and I have categorized them according to what they do best, or what best illustrates the point I want to make.

Chapter 1 examines packs that are designed to protect their contents from environmental damage through impact and exposure, as well as uncovering the ways in which they protect consumers, manufacturers, retailers and distributors from harm or liability if the packs or their contents are misused.

Chapter 2 describes packs that preserve the potency, integrity and life of their contents and their local, regional and national heritage, culture and traditions.

The subject of chapter 3 is how packs literally perform whether dramatically, ergonomically or environmentally.

Brands are the predominant theme of chapter 4 where they are shown to promote a company's identity and ideology, as well as give solid form and tangible value to inherently insubstantial products.

This book is therefore an overview of a broad area of design practice that has evolved to become a devastatingly fast and effective conduit between businesses and consumers. This exciting multi-channel medium communicates visually and verbally, directly and subliminally, in two and three dimensions to powerfully persuade us to think, buy, act and enjoy.

Protect

WELCOME TO THE
WORLD OF
ESTABLISHED & SONS

01   Established & Sons,
by MadeThought, UK, 2007.
Simple outer cartons protect and
preserve their contents and perform as
an exhibition structure that promotes
the company and its products.

Overview
Packaging
that Protects

Packaging design evolved with industrialization, commercialization and the growth of trade. What started out as a way of protecting an item from impact-related damage or environmental exposure grew in sophistication to include a broader definition of protection and, by association, 'responsibility'. In addition to keeping their contents safe today's packs also protect the manufacturer, distributor, retailer and user – physically and legally – from the consequences of misuse. They do this with overt and covert messages that control how the contents are transported, stored, unwrapped, displayed, tracked, deployed, dispensed, consumed, reused, recycled or trashed.

Overt messages include warnings and key information such as 'this way up', 'fragile', 'it takes two people to lift this crate', 'biohazard', or 'vegetarian'. They are usually verbal or communicated through pictorial symbols. Statutory legal information, which varies from country to country (how cosmopolitan!), is often tightly typeset in a very small size, and provides a visual texture that we rarely read but which we subliminally regard as a reassuring endorsement of integrity and authenticity. On food packs this legal jargon extends beyond the comprehensible ingredients to include chemical additives, E-numbers, places of origin and sometimes information about the ethical context within which the ingredients have been procured and what this procurement has involved. Food packs also try to protect us from ourselves by telling us how many calories and how much fat, protein, salt, carbohydrate and fibre we eat in a variety of simple and not-so-simple ways. At least theoretically, all this information helps us to protect our bodies, our beliefs and our values. Other packs try to save us from harm by telling us what not to ingest or touch, the cancerous implications of our habits or what kind of help to seek if we've ignored the warnings (assuming we're not now blind or dead). It's pretty remarkable that much of this information can fit on something as small as a cigarette packet or a sweet wrapper, in addition to the branding and the name of the product.

Covert messages are inherently subtle and often intuitive and use techniques such as tamperproof seals and other physical thresholds to protect us from inadvertent use by making us stop, think and act. Simply ensuring that type can be easily read when the pack is held the right way up prevents accidents from happening and pack contents from being spilled or damaged.

Today's packs protect their contents in countless ways. Some use old or new materials that are designed to collapse or destruct and absorb potentially harmful energy, in order to mitigate the effects of an explosion or accidental damage. Others provide protection against the effects of gases, liquids, electricity, radiation, micro-organisms, temperature, humidity, biological and chemical contamination, pressure, the environment or tampering by meddlesome creatures (including children, fungi, criminals and terrorists). There's a pack to protect every conceivable product in every imaginable situation.

The process of unwrapping a pack is often exploited in order to add a temporal dimension – and another aspect of protection – to its design. Obstacles that slow us down are also designed to create suspense and drama that add additional meaning and distinctiveness to the contents of the pack. Prestigious, sophisticated and expensive products should be savoured and appreciated, and through the unwrapping ritual packaging is used to emphasize and protect the value of goods in ways that go far beyond mere physical protection. The process of unwrapping is also sometimes used to deliver measured doses of medicine or stage-by-stage information about the contents of a pack, preventing us rushing ahead and tearing it open only to damage the contents, the product warranty and ourselves. For example, adhesive closures placed in our path make us pay attention to information; they operate like thresholds, saying 'Read me before you break me' because, as Alice in Wonderland discovered, there's no going back. Whether it's a legal agreement with a software company or your consumer rights in relation to a packet of hair dye, torn, peeled, opened and unwrapped means 'I do'.

01   Levi's® tissue wrap, by Checkland Kindleysides, UK, 2005. The value of these premium products is protected by the ritual of packaging them in tissue and further reinforced typographically explaining the product's heritage.

02   Levi's® carrier bags, by Checkland Kindleysides, UK, 2005. Carrier bags protect the buyer's sartorial reputation and provide environmental protection.

03   Shit Happens dog poo bags, by Nina Dautzenberg & Andrea Gadesmann, Junge Schachtel, Germany, 2008. These funky packs protect our environment, our health and our noses.

04   Chilli Berry Jelly, by Marks & Spencer, UK, 2006–7. Less is more because simple typographic craftsmanship increases the value of this product.

05   Essenz Vanilla Sugar-free flavouring syrup, by Graven Images, UK, 2007. Crystal-clear plastic looks like glass and protects from impact damage while decoration and synthetic heritage add credibility and value.

03

01

02

04

05

07   Magnanni shoe box,
by Pati Núñez, Spain, 2005.
Photography transforms this
protective shoe box into a
covetable conceptual artwork.

08   Prosays' Skincare, by
Tommy Li Design, China, 2006.
These metallic cosmetic compacts
protect by looking tough and precious.

09   Gift boxes, by Hermès,
France, 2007. Hermès iconic packs
combine luxurious materials with
anti-counterfeit measures.

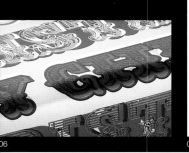

06

07

09

08

KSHOCOLÂT

20
BELGIAN
CHOCOLATES

Net Weight 260g/9.1oz

01   Kshocolât 20 Belgian
Chocolates box. Crafted modern
typography and layout add value to
an otherwise generic package.

02   Kshocolât Gift Tubes: Mini
Strawberrettes, Mini Pineapplettes,
Mini Orangettes. Unusual pack shapes,
simple compositions and strong colours
strongly differentiate Kshocolât's
products in the marketplace.

02

Case Study
Kshocolât chocolate bars

01

Pack	Kshocolât chocolate bars
Client	Kshocolât, UK
Designer	Marque, UK
Year	2007

While packaging for chocolate bars is legally required to include product information it doesn't need lots of additional material or complicated technology in order to effectively protect its contents. This gives the designer an excellent opportunity to show how design can add value to an otherwise ordinary range of packs.

For this handsome range of chocolate bars economical techniques were used to transform the wrapper and change the product from an ordinary commodity into a valuable gift or treat.

Made with only an uncoated recyclable paper outer wrapper, and a laminated aluminium foil and paper inner wrapper, these packs fill a gap in the market for chocolate products aimed at young and sophisticated consumers who are not attracted to more traditional chocolate-box packs.

Kshocolât's bars look special and expensive because more has been done with less. They command more money because they reduce visual clutter, use less material and processes that consume energy and resources, and do so without being self-righteously green.

Additional materials and decoration would detract from the crafted sans serif type that is carefully anchored against an imaginary left-hand margin. This tightens up an otherwise sparse layout and makes it appear as a tense single unit where each design element balances the composition and makes the whole pack appear satisfyingly complete. The consistent typographic approach and rich dark-coloured band at the bottom of each wrapper evokes chocolate and confirms that the packs are part of a range. Each flavour is characterized by a single carefully selected colour that expresses the variety: icy blue to suggest the coolness of milk in a dairy, dirty citrus yellow to describe lemon and pepper, and lavender-pink to conjure up rich nectar-bearing blossom and therefore honey. The colours are also 'soft', like the flavour and texture of chocolate.

Interview with Simon Coyle, *CEO, Kshocolât*

How do you describe the packaging?
The first word that springs to mind is 'simple' – chocolate as a gift product would have been too complicated and fussy in comparison to any other sort of gift.

Our products are very high quality, but this is not as unique as the way we present them, to appeal to a younger audience – although they do appeal to a wider audience than we had first expected.

What's special about it?
Simple can be difficult and it probably would have been easy for us to pick the first thing that was shown to us – the special thing was a long drawn-out process that ended with something that looks like it should have taken five minutes. The people and the process made the packaging.

How did you manage research and development?
A lot of it came out of the initial design process where we spent a lot of time thinking about the type of product we wanted.

01   Kshocolât's Hot Choc
range of 100% Real Chocolate Pure
Indulgence. Metal canisters communicate
that these are premium gift packs
that subvert the traditional decorative
approach to chocolate box design.

01

How long did it take to develop the initial idea?
It probably took about three or four months. But it is still evolving.

What is the catalyst for evolving the design?
We have a strong gift market but we wanted to increase our market for impulse-buy entry-level products so we could raise brand awareness and utilize some of the retail chain channels. So it was commercially driven.

How important is packaging to you?
I always want to say it's the most important thing that we have. We have never once had to pitch for anything, other than present our product and let customers take it. The product itself – luxury chocolate – is a given. You use the finest ingredients, the right flavours, but at the end of the day what people see is the presentation of Kshocolât. And the packaging couldn't be any more important to our brand given the ultra-premium nature of our market.

Interview with Hector Pottie,
Creative Director, Marque

How did the project begin?
It was about the design, it was about the packaging and it was about the idea that you could buy a gift for yourself. And it was likened to perfume packaging where perfume's one of the things that you might buy for yourself as a little treat. So… leading from a design perspective, making it minimal – just the name on the outside, really strong colours, really, really simple designs. It's about the ceremony of opening it as much as it is about the chocolate itself.

02   Kshocolât Peppermint Creams. This pack's unconventional colour hints at the product's flavour but also subverts the genre by being hard-edged and modern rather than softly romantic.

03   Kshocolât Impulse Bags: Mini Strawberrettes, Chilli Almonds, Mini Orangettes, Dark Almonds. These tiny hand-sized mini-packs are glossy, black and sexy.

03

02

How successful were the new packs? In the first year after the new packs were launched sales went up 1,500 per cent. They went from selling in just one little outlet to over 1,000 stores. It was great – really successful.

How did you choose the paper stock? A lot of it was chosen by the client. We said we wanted an uncoated stock. There are production restrictions – we make it cost-effective by printing in two spot colours, which suits the simple design.

01　　　　Kshocolât's range of chocolate bars. These everyday products are special because of their reductive, subversive, carefully crafted design and fashionable off-beat colours.

02　　　　Dining Chocolates. After-dinner chocolates are modernized and made fashionable by this striking typographic packaging that is sure to initiate dinner party discussions.

DINING CHOCOLATES
ORANGE & CARDAMOM
DARK CHOCOLATE
HONEYCOMB & VANILLA
LEMON & PEPPER
MILK CHOCOLATE

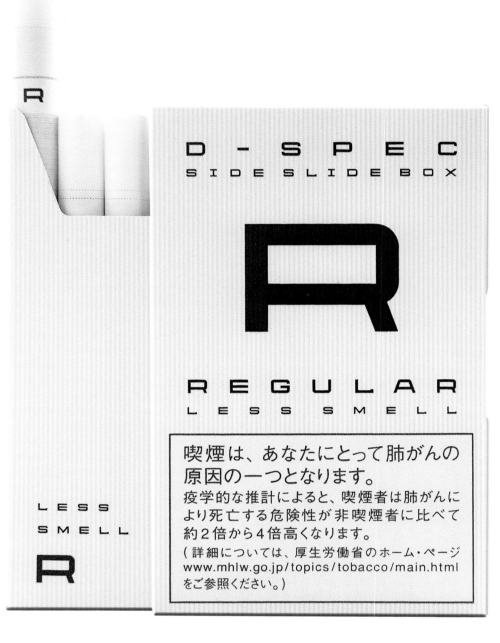

D-SPEC
SIDE SLIDE BOX

R

REGULAR
LESS SMELL

LESS
SMELL

R

喫煙は、あなたにとって肺がんの
原因の一つとなります。
疫学的な推計によると、喫煙者は肺がんに
より死亡する危険性が非喫煙者に比べて
約２倍から４倍高くなります。
(詳細については、厚生労働省のホーム・ページ
www.mhlw.go.jp/topics/tobacco/main.html
をご参照ください。)

02

Pack   **Alphabet Heavy,
          Coolmint and
          Regular filter cigarettes**
Client   **Japan Tobacco
          International, Japan**
Designer **Asyl, Japan**
Year   **2004**

These cardboard cigarette cartons illustrate perfectly how smoking can be stylish as well as deadly.

The elegant packs are a design exercise in how to do more with less. Less surface decoration means that more effort is invested in crafting the card pack and imbuing its few elements with meaning and value. A bespoke letter C indicates Coolmint, R is for Regular and H for Heavy. Colours express the international language of flavour and strength while type communicates and decorates every part of the pack, including the product and health warning, to deliver a single, homogeneous essay in understated style. The packs are accessorized with a range of Zippo cigarette lighters.

The cigarettes are protected from impact by a card box-within-a-box construction that demonstrates the designer's understanding of smoking etiquette and cigarette sharing. The outer box creates a sliding inner tray that can be pushed open with the thumb to politely offer the cigarettes. This gesture dramatizes and glamorizes the event, and evokes the expensive cigarette containers that were popular in the early twentieth century.

While smokers will be reassured by the familiar pack size, they will also be amused by the design of the sliding tray, which echoes the silhouette of the cut-out area of a standard rigid cigarette carton.

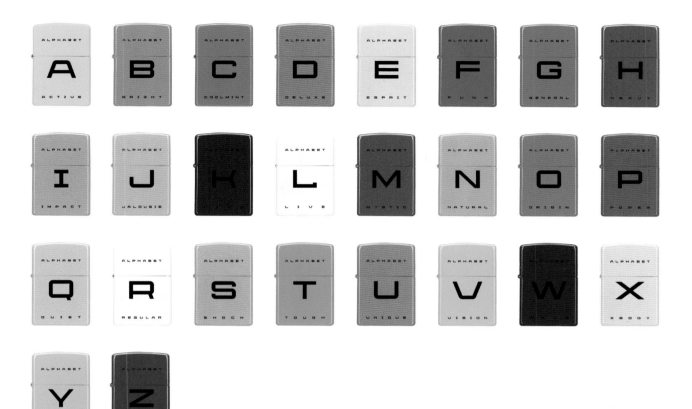

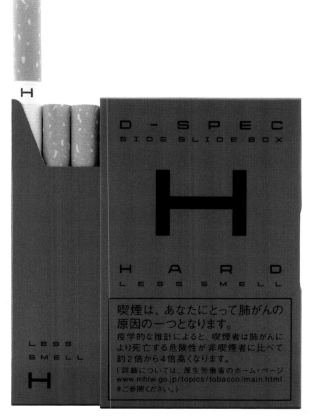

03

Pack   Tesco Ingredients range
Client   Tesco, UK
Designer   Wes Anson, with Creative
            Directors Simon
            Pemberton and Adrian
            Whitefoord, P&W Design
            Consultants, UK
Year   2007

These packs protect in four different ways. Firstly, they are designed to make basic cookery ingredients as appealing as attractively packaged ready-made meals, thereby encouraging people to protect their well-being by experimenting with healthy home cookery rather than buying pre-prepared food.

Secondly, different culinary traditions are protected by helping people to cook with ingredients that span, for example, Chinese, English and Italian cultures. The packs also use illustrations and text inspired by contemporary cookery books and recipe cards, reinforcing the link in consumers' minds between the ingredients and the dishes.

Thirdly, each pack protects the integrity of its product by being the right one for the job: sea salt in a glass preserving jar, vinegar in a tall glass bottle, vanilla pods in an aluminium 'cigar case' – traditional containers that, in turn, protect the environment because they are reusable or recyclable.

Lastly, packaging products in formats that are too attractive to hide behind cupboard doors means the consumer can create a professional-looking kitchen that protects and conserves the traditional idea of a pantry.

04

Pack   **Target ClearRX bottles**
Client   **Target ClearRX, USA**
Designer **Deborah Adler, USA**
Year   **2005**

When Deborah Adler's grandmother accidentally consumed her grandfather's medicine the designer decided to redesign pharmacy packaging 'from the bottle up' to protect users against the possibility of misusing prescribed drugs.

Her ClearRX system, developed in conjunction with Target, uses a new bottle shape, made from polyethylene terephthalate plastic, that is easily gripped and opened. Its flat faces ensure that graphic information is clearly displayed and mean that there is no need to turn the bottle round to read the text. An optional oral syringe enables liquids to be accurately and easily measured.

The easy-to-read adhesive paper labels have straightforward instructions typeset in Myriad, which is legible at small sizes, and new icons make important medical warnings comprehensible. Prescription information is also reorganized with vital information, including the drug's name and user instructions, at the top. An additional label allows packs to be identified when they are organized in a drawer. The colour-coded rings on the bottle's neck identify each person's medication and prevent people taking a medicine intended for another family member.

A patient information card that summarizes common uses and side effects is tucked into a sleeve on the bottle's reverse and functions as a quick reference – it is accompanied by a free magnifier to ensure that all information is as legible as possible.

& Co.

TIFFANY

01   Tiffany & Co.'s carrier bags. Tiffany's celebrated blue packs validate and protect the expense and status of their contents.

02   The interiors of these gift boxes are dyed to perfectly match their exteriors.

Case Study
Tiffany & Co. boxes and bags

02

05

Pack   **Tiffany & Co. boxes and bags**
Client   **Tiffany & Co., USA**
Designer   **Paula Scher, Pentagram Design, USA**
Year   **2003**

The iconic blue boxes and bags of the legendary United States jeweller Tiffany & Co. have become a metaphor for celebrity luxury. Their strong colour, carefully crafted design and familiar typographic style have established them as internationally recognized classics that have endured for over 170 years.

The packs are special for more than just the longevity of their simple design. Their apparently weak materials, including acid-free paper and card, are engineered to increase the impact of, and provide some environmental protection for, the valuable objects – often made from precious metals and diamonds – they contain. They achieve both these things while also functioning as the cornerstone of Tiffany & Co.'s brand, and delivering sensual pleasure to the company's customers.

The recent evolution of the packs simultaneously protects the heritage of Tiffany & Co. and modernizes it in order to attract new, young and affluent patrons.

Interview with Paula Scher, *Principal, Pentagram Design USA*

What is special about a Tiffany & Co. box?
Tiffany & Co. already had Tiffany Blue but they didn't have a very nice paper stock. We changed the colours. The typography was very large scale on the box and we made it simple and delicate. And you see the blue and you recognize the box and you see the typography and it's small so that it looks like it's engraved and the paper has a kind of a softness to it. The goal was to make it special!

It's a very old brand – has it drifted over time?
It isn't that it's drifted. Tiffany never consciously branded their packaging. It was developed over time by the people that manufactured the jewellery. They picked blue at one point. The Tiffany logo is a font that originally came from a typesetter.

That must have been a lovely opportunity – to take a piece of typography that evolved over generations and make it perfect.
That's what the whole project was about. We had Jonathan

Hoefler redraw the type so it would look as if the packages were engraved. Type was scaled specifically for each individual box. It creates a certain kind of proportion and that's what you see when you see the advertising as well.

What did you design into the 'out-of-box-experience'?
The paper for the box is very important because you touch it and savour it, even though there's another more permanent jewel box in there that contains the ring or diamond necklace, and is not as distinctive as the Tiffany gift box – you recognize the colour and you get excited because you know what's inside. The paper had to feel expensive: that somebody cared enough to wrap the box. We dyed the insides of all the boxes so they matched the paper, so that you… had this very exclusive box that was part of the process and part of the gift.

Who worked on this project?
Just me and two designers – Keith Daigle and Anka Stolman. It was over a couple of years.

01   Detail of cord carrier bag handles. The appearance and 'feel' of the cord was carefully considered as part of the design process.

02   Gift boxes. Typography was reduced in size to express the fragile, precious qualities of the company's products.

03   The composition of the company's visual identity is derived from its iconic packaging.

04   Tiffany & Co. book. The design of this publication features typography and colour derived from the company's iconic packaging.

05   Carrier bag and box. The proportions of type to blue area are the same in both boxes and carrier bags.

02

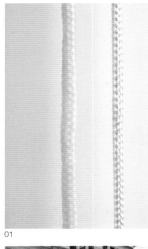

01

03

04

Did you involve customers in the box designs?
We talked to everybody in the store about how they worked with their customers. Because it's about having the experience of Tiffany – being able to see your box wrapped.

What's the relationship between the box and the bag?
They're the same material and the same scale of typography. Tiffany are a courageous client to be able to know that their blue was signature enough and that you could put the logo really small on the bag. Everybody wants their shopping bag to be their flag and people want their logos really big on them. Tiffany knew they had their flag in the blue.

What else was unusual about this project?
It was unusual for me because it required total restraint. It looked so much like Tiffany and so little like me! The idea of having to really hold back in favour of this thing that had a life of its own was really interesting – I've never really done that. What existed in that brand and the brand heritage is what every company wants. So it was actually amazing to me that they had gone so many years without any kind of real professional help with the packaging, because they really didn't need it all that much. They needed to turn up the volume a little on the quality side but they had done so much right from the beginning, like holding on to a colour. I can't imagine most businesses saying 'This is our colour and we're never changing it'. It's very hard for organizations to do that.

06

Pack   **Cohiba Mini cigarillos**
Client   **Cohiba, Cuba**
Designer   **Cohiba, Cuba**
Year   **2007**

While the tightly fitting lid and high-quality craftsmanship of this card and paper pack prevent cigarillos being squashed, they also create an exceptional design icon. The excellent printing, aluminium foiling, embossing and paper engineering create a pack that functions impeccably and has the fit and finish appropriate for this premium product.

The name Cohiba is derived from the word the 'Taino', the original inhabitants of Cuba used to describe tobacco, hence the golden tribal head. While black-and-white checks and egg-yolk orange may mean danger, this brand originated in the 1960s when such elements were fashionable.

Opening the flip-top lid produces a welcoming gesture that invites sharing. The logotype on the inner lid ensures that the brand is seen and the value of the gift acknowledged. The paper cover restates the logotype and provides a dramatic pause before the curtain is lifted and the main act – the cigarillos – is revealed. In the journey from the outer pack to the inner pack and product this box reveals a perfect little drama that builds to deliver a satisfying, and very stylish, conclusion.

Ideologically, the pack originates in a time and place far removed from the mundanity of health warnings, which are simply applied as stickers like a legal Band-Aid.

07

Pack   **Arroz Sivaris rice tubes**
Client   **NM Arrossos**
            de Qualitat, Spain
Designer   **Pepe Gimeno, Spain**
Year   **2006**

Sivaris is a family business in Valencia, dedicated to the cultivation, production and selling of rice.

These packs protect in several different ways. The wound-card tube provides a strong container that prevents the contents being damaged by impact while the inner polythene bag both reveals the rice and protects it from moisture.

The environment is also protected – by a frugal design approach to materials and production. Off-the-shelf tubes and caps are recyclable and reusable, and contrast beautifully with the texture of the rice grains to express the product's natural origins and the environmental and sustainable aspects of growing rice.

Production processes were kept to a minimum in order to save energy and money. Graphics are simply laser-printed on to the Kraft paper that is glued around the tubes. Single colours are used to distinguish between the different varieties of rice in the range and prevent customer confusion. This economical, minimal and modern approach is continued in the decorative san serif typography, to create a range of high-quality packs that cost-effectively raise the status of the gourmet products they contain and increase their retail value. Because the packs are tube-shaped they also have the advantage of differentiating Sivaris rice from that of its competitors, which is normally sold in bags or rectangular boxes.

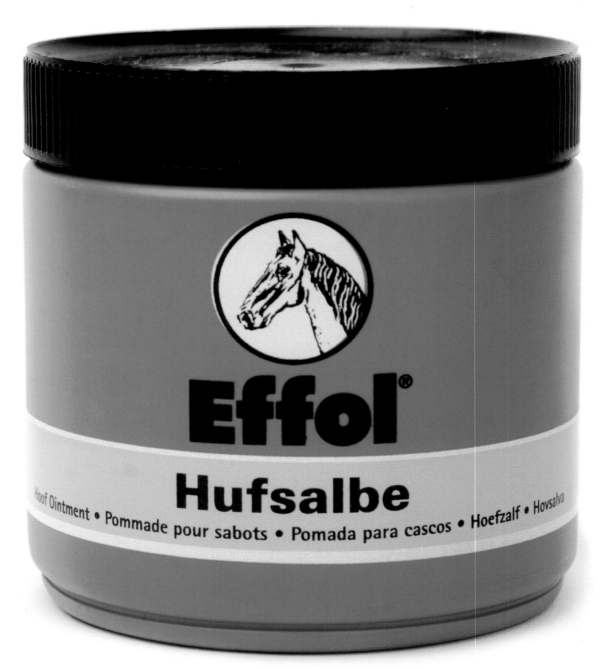

08

Pack　　Effol Hufsalbe
Client　　Schweizer Effax,
　　　　　Germany
Designer　Schweizer Effax,
　　　　　Germany
Year　　　2007

This pack of ointment for horses' hooves protects its contents from impact and misuse. It also protects the no-nonsense credibility of the agricultural sector – and therefore the efficacy of the product.

　　　The pliable polypropylene plastic tub is unbreakable, durable and manly, and evokes big, rugged and green-coloured outdoor brands like John Deere. The hefty industrial Helvetica sans serif typeface suggests that horses are more 'engineering' than equine, and the illustration shows a proud stallion rather than a pretty mare!

　　　But this is no ordinary agricultural pack. The tub is beautifully proportioned as well as easy to grip and use. The graphic layout is simple, ordered and communicative. Even the bright yellow band with black type has a discreet white border that illuminates the panel, drawing the eye to the superlegible product description, so that the pack can quickly be found on a cluttered shelf or in a dark corner. Just in case a customer doesn't see the type and thinks the product might be for their tractor, the bright illustration of the horse makes it clear that it's not. Unlike some packs, this one perfectly complements its contents: a dense, matt, purple-black lubricant for horses that smells of both thyme and tar.

Pack　　　　**Hermès boxes**
Client　　　 **Hermès, France**
Designer　**Hermès, France**
Year　　　　**2007**

Some of the world's most iconic packs were created by accident, and Hermès' orange colour originated during the occupation of France in the Second World War. The company ran out of the pale beige paper it used and the only available replacement was orange. Today Hermès' signature orange boxes are synonymous with luxury throughout the world.

Like many manufacturers of luxury goods, the company protects its packaging and products from counterfeiting by incorporating unique details that are difficult and expensive for criminals to copy. While the orange boxes are sufficiently robust to protect their valuable contents, and endure as collectable keepsakes, the card boxes are comparatively easy to copy. Hermès' in-house editions department therefore constantly evolves the design of its inner packs to make them more difficult to counterfeit.

Historically, within each box, the product was contained in a woven cotton bag made from plain brown-coloured fabric printed with the Hermès Calèche (carriage) logotype. These have now been replaced by a unique herringbone-patterned woven fabric, Toilesh, that is a variety of toile exclusive to Hermès and was developed by the company in order to create a fabric that is technically difficult and expensive to copy.

01   CrushPak is used to package Fresh 'n' Fruity Splatz. Its innovative delivery mechanism protects clothes and fingers from mess and allows us to consume food cleanly without the need for cutlery.

02   Fresh 'n' Fruity Splatz flavoured yoghurt pots. CrushPak is manufactured using existing equipment and standard materials.

Case Study
EverEdgeIP CrushPak

02

10

Pack   EverEdgeIP CrushPak
Client   Fonterra, New Zealand
Designer   EverEdgeIP,
            New Zealand
Year   2005

EverEdgeIP is an industrial design and product-marketing business that develops and licenses patented technologies such as CrushPak. This ground-breaking product takes advantage of the trend for convenience dining – eating any time, any place, anywhere – to create a new way of consuming everyday foods like yoghurt.

Instead of simply containing and protecting the product, CrushPak capitalizes on our tendency to destroy packs that frustrate us, such as plastic yoghurt pots with awkward corners that are wasteful because they stop us from consuming all their contents and make our fingers and faces messy.

CrushPak subverts table manners and changes the way we eat by encouraging us to crush plastic yoghurt-type pots in a controlled way in order to consume their contents. The satisfyingly destructive process collapses them in concertina-like folds that expel the product and clean the pot, thereby reducing product waste. It also folds the empty polypropylene pack so it uses less space in the recycling bin, where it can be recycled up to 50 times. CrushPak ensures that consumers stay clean while enjoying messy foods without the need for a spoon. And anything with a viscous, gelatinous or thick consistency can be delivered in an easy-to-use, low-waste pack.

As well as being convenient and intuitive for consumers to use, industrialists like CrushPak because it is made with smaller quantities of standard material than conventional packs, and is manufactured using existing machinery rather than requiring capital expenditure on new equipment.

While CrushPak revitalizes existing products such as yoghurt, it can also be used to create new markets and brands by allowing other messy, viscous foods, such as pastes, sauces, soups and condiments, to be consumed on the move. And CrushPak's not just for food – it can be used for non-food products too, such as paint.

Interview with Paul Adams, CEO, EverEdgeIP

How do you describe CrushPak?
CrushPak is a compressible pack that enables the user to consume the contents in different ways. They can either squeeze the pack together and consume the contents straight from the pack without a spoon, or they can use a spoon, or they can use it as a dispenser, for example, to squeeze paint into a pot.

What is so great about CrushPak?
The 'different ways to consume' is regarded advantageously by companies as it means they can position their products in a way they couldn't before.

Were you interested in reducing product waste?
A key consideration was to design it so there was zero product waste whether using a spoon or not. We wanted to make sure that it was different from a traditional pack that you use with a spoon so people didn't feel like they were getting ripped off. We wanted the consumer to feel that they could get all the product out.

01 Design development sketch. Many different shapes were considered during the design development process.

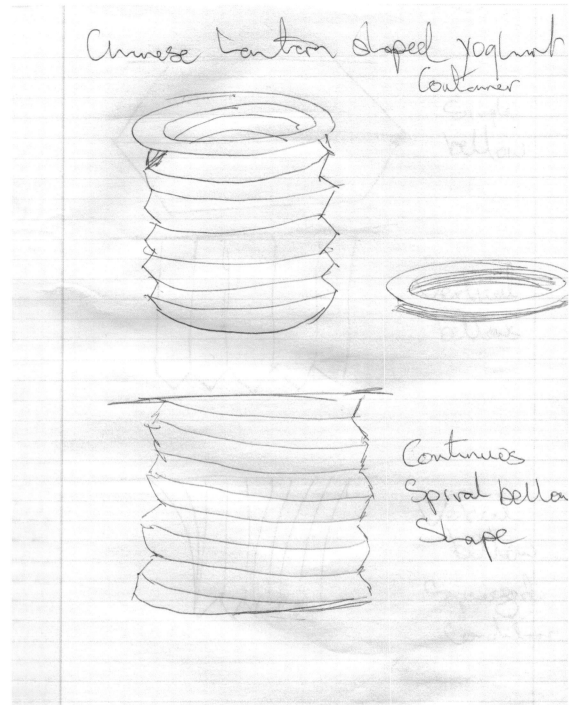

Chinese Lantern shaped yoghurt Container

Continues Spiral bellow Shape

01

Where did the idea for CrushPak come from?
It was from Michael Kessel who works here at EverEdgeIP. He was sitting in his neighbour's kitchen having a chat, and the neighbour's four-year-old child opened the fridge and grabbed a traditional pot of yoghurt – a single pot – and squashed it and literally tried to drink the yoghurt out of the pot. It burst and ran everywhere. He picked it up and said, 'You know, there has got to be a better way of doing this'.

How long did CrushPak take to develop?
The initial concept was developed in May 2003 and we considered patenting a relatively final version in December 2004. So that was about 18 months of development. And then we did a further six months of commercial development to take it through to June 2005 when we first presented it to Fonterra [the world's largest dairy cooperative based in New Zealand] and a number of others. So June 2005 was the end of the formal development period – but

we have been working on further development for another two-year period.

How many people and industries worked on CrushPak's development?
Many different people – half a dozen within our team. We spoke to folk from packaging industries and we did a fair amount of rapid prototyping. Then we did extensive industrial testing – and market testing. And some design companies gave their opinions as to how we should present things.

02   Design development sketch of collapsible 'bellows'. The merits of horizontal and vertical bellows were explored in order to determine the most effective pack solution.

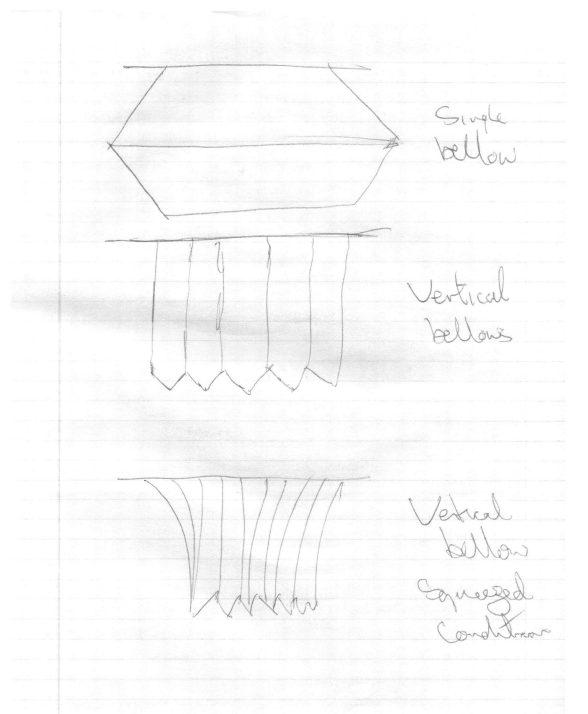

Single bellow

Vertical bellows

Vertical bellow

Squeezed Condition

02

How did you ensure that the pack collapsed in the correct way and didn't deform, break or split? Was that a big part of your research?
Yes it was. We were very focused on ensuring that the pack would fit with one of Fonterra's existing manufacturing lines. Fonterra put a lot of research into their own conventional packs to make sure the material did not split at certain temperatures etc. CrushPak proved remarkably forgiving because we didn't have to use a special type of plastic.

01   CAD render of final pack
from below. The final design solution
optimized the amount of product
that could be expelled from the pack
and consumed without causing
the plastic to crack or break.

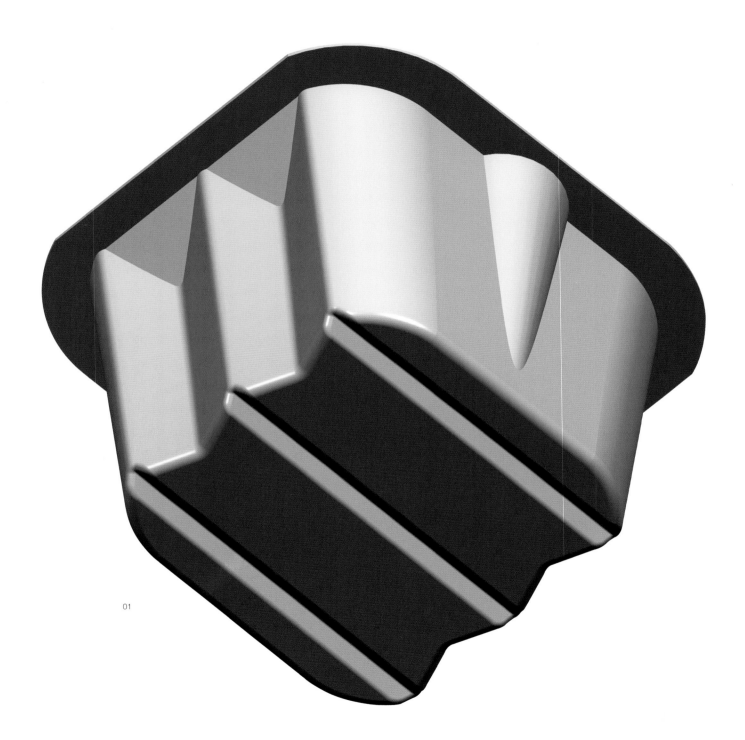

01

02   CrushPak during use. The
contents can be expelled from the pack
and consumed without causing mess.

03   CrushPak after being
used. CrushPak maximizes the amount
of product that can be consumed
thereby minimizing waste.

03

02

11

Pack   Kiehl's Creme de Corps
Client   Kiehl's, USA
Designer Kiehl's Creative Studio,
          USA
Year   2007

Detailed and dense typographical lists of ingredients and old-fashioned words like 'efficacious' reflect Kiehl's medicinal beginnings as a pharmacy, established in New York over 150 years ago.

Kiehl's values its heritage. The company also takes its product-related facts, advice and ingredients, and their effects on consumers, very seriously. Instead of being relegated to the reverse label, or hidden in an accompanying leaflet, they dominate the packaging, where they deliver two different kinds of potent protection. Firstly, the scientific-sounding words protect Kiehl's pharmaceutical credibility and reassure consumers that the products actually work. Secondly,

by revealing each product's constituent parts the company encourages customers to trust the brand and use the information to protect themselves from adverse allergic or ideological reactions to any of the ingredients – which builds loyalty. Historically, the pharmacist would have delivered this information verbally, and Kiehl's labels maintain the tradition by being talkative, helpful and knowledgeable.

White is also a feature of Kiehl's packs, perhaps recalling the apothecary's porcelain containers and aseptic environment, and aligning the brand with the efficacy of the medical profession. The logotype in nineteenth-century commercial script is the only

decoration on the packs; otherwise they rely on the monochromatic decorative texture of sans serif typography, with the occasional product name highlighted in red.

12

Pack   **Chocolate Abyss
            drinking chocolate**
Client   **Espresso Warehouse,
            UK**
Designer   **Graven Images, UK**
Year   **2007**

This pack uses design to protect its contents from impact and environmental exposure, express product credentials and add value to an otherwise off-the-shelf range of containers.

Stock polyurethane lids, composite cardboard and steel tins with foil bags are transformed into handsome packaging for luxury drinking chocolate. The tins are constructed in a spiral for strength and foil-lined to repel moisture, and the chocolate powder is sealed with foil to protect it from environmental gases and tampering, as well as moisture. The bright orange lids are durable and will not crack, break or tear, and attract the customer's eye.

As the name suggests, the product is aimed at adults who take their drinking chocolate as seriously as their coffee, and demand that it is organic, ethically sourced and contains real chocolate – expressed by the bespoke 'percentage cocoa' symbol.

The outcome is an industrially chic pack that uses product facts and certifications, a lyrical 'deeper, darker' product description, rich chocolate-colour palette and grown-up undecorated sans serif type to express luxury, quality and integrity in straight-forward ways. Decoration is not used to compensate for low product quality; instead it supports the product description and helps the chocolate to speak for itself.

13

Pack **Dr. Bronner's Magic Soaps**
Client **Dr. Bronner's, USA**
Designer **Dr. Bronner's, USA**
Year **2008**

Dr. Bronner's soap bars are unique because they aim to cleanse the minds of their users, as well as their bodies, in order to unite and protect the earth's 6 billion inhabitants. In addition to proclaiming their organic, fairtrade and environmental credentials the packaging is also crammed with information about Dr. Bronner's personal philosophy.

In the 1950s, when he found that people would buy his soap but not listen to his speeches, Dr. Bronner began to print his philosophy on soap wrappers, and throughout the 1960s countercultural hippy revolution, these became his soapbox – a practice that his family continues today in innovative, socially responsible ways that support progressive causes and charities.

In addition to protecting the soaps from impact and environmental damage, the single-coloured card and paper wrappers have an unusual typographic design that contrasts strongly with the softer, more feminine or illustrative packs of the company's competitors. The soaps' certified natural products, and their strident ecological, humanist and humanitarian ethos, have established them as the top-selling natural soap brands in the United States and Japan.

This new range of organic products celebrates the company's 60th anniversary, and its new status as the largest personal care company certified by the United States Drug Administration's National Organic Program.

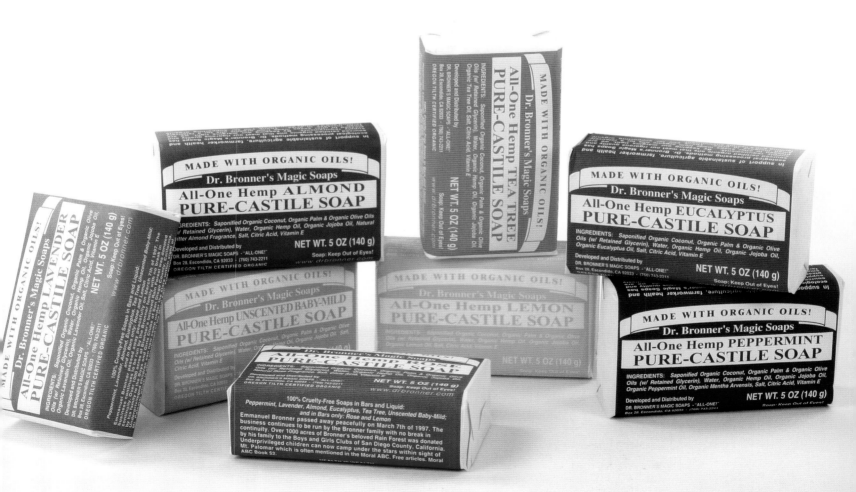

14

Pack Scotia Seeds
Client Scotia Seeds, UK
Designer Giles Laverack,
Scotia Seeds, UK
Year 2007

These packs look distinctively different compared to other more colourful and commercial-looking seed packs. They are special because they deliver three kinds of protection to help safeguard the rare wild flowers whose seeds they contain.

Firstly, the packs protect the seeds from deteriorating or germinating through contact with moisture and light by sealing them in aluminium foil inner packs. Secondly, they protect horticultural tradition by enclosing the inner pack in an old-fashioned, striped kraft paper outer envelope that looks like the brown paper envelopes which old-fashioned, or professional gardeners use to dry and store seeds.

The stencilled style of the type capitalizes on the same tradition, by reinforcing the handmade and hand-gathered ethos of plant collecting in the field, while the flower's name, in both English and Latin, precedes and dominates its picture – hinting that the product is more of an academic exercise in plant conservation than simply selling seeds.

Thirdly, this modest pack, with its studious low-tech aesthetic, has the feel of a real potting shed with stencilled seed trays and plant labels, encouraging customers to believe that by buying and sowing these rare seeds in their own gardens they will help protect and conserve wild plant species.

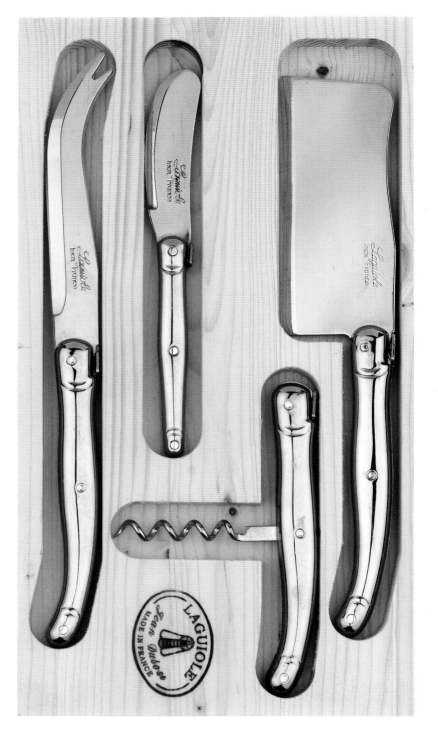

15

Pack   **Laguiole wine and**
            cheese set
Client   **Laguiole, France/**
            Habitat, UK
Designer   **Jean Dubost, France**
Year   **2007**

These traditional Laguiole cheese knives and corkscrew are robustly packaged in a unique single-sided softwood case, to protect them from impact during warehousing and transit, and make them easy to stack and attractive to display.

Cutlery has been produced in the small town of Laguiole near Thiers in France since 1829, and the cases protect the authenticity of the products by allowing customers to see the bumble bee trademark engraved on each blade and branded on the pack.

This regional emblem is present on all original Laguiole cutlery and proves it is genuine. The area's knife-making skills incorporate many wood-based processes, including the branding and routing techniques featured in the pack.

Each knife fits comfortably within a machine-routed space that prevents the high-grade stainless-steel blades rubbing together and damaging the other products. The knives are held in place by shrink-wrapped plastic – an unlikely but appropriate low-tech solution.

Creating this pack from a single piece of inexpensive, lightweight softwood with the machinery used to manufacture the products is both cost effective and environmentally beneficial. The pack is also reusable – as a container in which to keep and protect the knives, or as firewood!

MARKS &
SPENCER

lightly salted
beetroot crisps

from the field...

Beetroots make a colourful alternative
to potatoes when it comes to crisps.
We use the finest quality boro varietal
whole beetroots for these, because they
have the best flavour and richest colour.
They're simply sliced and flash cooked
in a little sunflower oil so all the sweet
beetroot taste comes through in every
beetroot crisp.

01　　　　Marks & Spencer Lightly
Salted Beetroot Crisps. Provenance
is clearly explained in order to inform
and protect the consumer.

02　　　　English Mint Jelly. Simple
clear product descriptions protect
the retailer–customer relationship by
preventing misunderstandings.

03　　　　Vintage Christmas Pudding.
This gift box protects the high value
of this luxury celebration pudding.

03

Case Study
Marks & Spencer speciality range

02

16

Pack　　　Marks & Spencer
　　　　　speciality range
Client　　Marks & Spencer, UK
Designer　Marks & Spencer, UK
Year　　　2006–7

This supermarket range is aimed at customers who are interested in the provenance and quality of their food, and who shop at farmers' markets. Each product has a special story to tell about its origins, craftsmanship, seasonality, ingredients or ethical sourcing and production methods.

The packs are designed to communicate the special characteristics of each product. They're also intended to look like a collection and to be collectable. They are premium products, signalled by the matt black and simple white modern typography that's roundly seriffed, direct and just a little paternalistic. Stories written on pack fronts reinforce the product's gourmet credentials while photography provides further seductive contextual information and evidence of origin.

The matt black and white colour palette makes these packs easy to find on the supermarket shelves. It provides an attractive and contrasting black frame that complements the photography and the products contained inside. It also acts as a buffer from other noisy packs that might be placed next to it

– the bright images against a dark background attract and hold the customer's eye. Black also heightens the colours in the photography and makes them look even more sumptuous.

Rather than adopting one homogeneous approach, each item is packaged using the method that best suits the product – jam and conserves in plain glass jars and biscuits in dark cardboard boxes. This means the range is varied, interesting and not wilfully overdesigned. The natural character of the products is always protected and expressed; this has the added benefit that new products can be cost effectively added to the range without the need for extensive redesign to make them fit.

At Christmas the range is given a subtle and sophisticated festive makeover with the addition of foil blocking and a little red or metallic ink.

This range 'protects' in one further fundamental way: it protects customers by arming them with information – educating them about where their food comes from and why it is good by explaining its history and its culinary and cultural value. While

some of this information is explained visually with photographs and controlled glimpses of the product, much is conveyed through text.

Spoken and written words play a big part in differentiating Marks & Spencer from other supermarkets. Products are named and explained – whether they're from the farm, the family dairy, the orchard, the charcuterie, the sea, or some other place like a saltmarsh. Then there is information about the product – where it comes from, what it's made of and how it tastes.

This helpful, but rather didactic tone of voice is balanced by the fashionable lower-case type and sophisticated overall appearance of the range.

01   Salt Marsh Lamb Half
Leg. Photography is used as 'proof' of
provenance and to evoke the rare, and
therefore high value, of the product.

02   Ravens Oak Goats Cheese.
Copy and photography explain the
unique context, and therefore protect
the high value, of this artisan product.

MARKS &
SPENCER

ravens oak goats cheese

from ravens oak dairy...
Handmade by Katy Hollinshead
in her small Cheshire farmhouse
dairy, this award-winning cheese
is made in small batches using
local milk. Curds are ladled by
hand into the moulds before
each cheese is carefully
turned, matured and
hand wrapped.

02

MARKS &
SPENCER

salt marsh
lamb half leg

01

Interview with Charlotte Raphael, *Senior Design Manager, Marks & Spencer*

Who decides what to call the product?
The product developers tell us exactly what the product is, and their proposed title, and then we tweak it so it fits in with the rest of the range.

How do you go about writing pack copy?
We have an internal copywriter as part of our design process.

I wondered if it was a female copywriter, because it just sounds like it's got a woman's touch about it?
Yes it does actually, that's true.

Who does she work with when writing copy?
She works with the designers and the product development team. The design obviously influences the tone – and the length – of the copy, while the product development team can fill in all the details of where the product's come from and what's particularly special about it.

Because there are lots of different people working in different departments to contribute to this range, how do you ensure that everything has the same look and feel?
With a project like this, which is really wide, we start with an overall brief from the head of product development. We pull together mood boards to show our proposed design route, then from there we can create a style guide, which lays out the design principles for the range. It covers the ethos, the customers we're aiming at, the photography style, type style and so on.

03   Bittersweet Orange
& Cranberry Marmalade. This
product's appetising and seasonal
colour are enhanced by the addition
of a simple festive label.

04   Greek Olives with Orange &
Peppers. Application of a seal reinforces
the high value of this premium product.

05   Elderflower Cordial. The
large areas of black used on the label
and neck seal of this glass bottle are
shorthand language for 'high quality'.

03

05

04

What role does the descriptive copy play within the overall Marks & Spencer brand? Descriptive copy helps customers to understand the product, and entices them to try it – it's our version of a menu, if you like. Different ranges may use different tones; our kids' food, for example, is very fun and irreverent, to tie in with the illustrated design route. With Speciality, we want customers to feel they're in a really great deli, or farmer's market, so the copy is informative, descriptive and very 'foodie' in its tone.

17

Pack   Rosie Fairtrade Tea
Client   Espresso Warehouse,
           UK
Designer   Graven Images, UK
Year   2007

The name of this product is derived from Cockney rhyming slang for tea – 'Rosie Lee' – reflecting its historical roots in the English tradition of tea-drinking. While the pack uses three physical layers of packaging to protect the product, the most potent form of 'protection' refers to its ethical certification which is encoded within its black, white and blue pattern.

Each layer of card and paper protection surrounding the tea features the same patterned decoration. Perforated-paper tea bags have patterned tags and card retail boxes are smothered in pattern. Even the bi-walled corrugated kraft card outer cartons that protect the retail boxes during transit from factory to shop are covered in pattern – indicating their dual role as promotional items in the retail environment.

The pattern is a modern version of the traditional willow pattern originally seen on Chinese-made porcelain produced for the British export market in the late eighteenth century. It is believed to tell the story of two doomed lovers who are eventually, and justly, reunited and immortalized as doves.

Espresso Warehouse has developed the pattern's central theme of justice by including a set of scales – its international symbol – and in doing so has proclaimed Rosie Tea's Fairtrade certification from carton to cup.

18

Pack   **Vintage Stila Eyeshadow**
Client   **Stila Cosmetics, USA**
Designer   **Stila Cosmetics, USA**
Year   **2007**

Stila has only been around since 1994, but in this short time it has used its packaging to reinforce and protect its unique market position as 'the thinking woman's choice' – packs include thought-provoking feminist quotations that urge users to question issues of feminism and skin-deep beauty.

Eyeshadows from the Vintage Stila range – vintage because the packs evoke simple, round cardboard face-powder containers from the 1940s – come in small, compact-style boxes that are startlingly different to the plethora of plastic containers used by the company's competitors. Card finished with matt silver foil both protects and complements the soft colours of the shimmering and matt eyeshadow powders. The underside of the lid is unfinished, recyclable brown card and is where the quotation is printed, typeset in an old-fashioned typewriter font. This gives the pack a subtle contemporary edge by being typeset in lower case.

19

Pack   Prosays' skincare range
Client   Prosays', Japan
Designer   Tommy Li Design, China
Year   2006

This new Japanese company produces a range of 30 skincare products aimed at women who are high or middle earners. The brand name means 'the professional says', and is calculated to appeal to professional women who expect skincare to perform because it is underpinned by objective input from other professionals, not simply because it carries a designer's signature.

Rather than hide behind patronizing packs that are pretty, colourful and decorative, and parody traditional femininity, Prosays' acknowledges women's changing roles by creating packaging that is handsome, classic, monochrome and looks professional.

Inner packs use a palette of reflective and translucent plastics and glass to provide discreet textural decoration that is more confident and adult than bright colours or ostentatious materials. Promotional text and information are organized in a workman-like grid layout.

Graphic decoration is restricted to matt-textured card outer cartons that provide protection against impact and shelf presence, and demonstrate a responsible attitude to the environment by being recyclable. Gritty, textural 'art photography' of insects (a stick insect decorates the pack of a camouflage product called Disappear), as well as plants and laboratory equipment,

expresses objectivity rather than emotion and describes ingredients or metaphorically explains product performance. The images are also contemporary and aspirational – and would look great on the boardroom wall.

20

Pack   **Storm Matches**
Client   **Loch Lomond and the**
            Trossachs National Park,
            UK/Lucy Byatt,
            The Centre, UK
Designer   **Olaf Nicolai, UK**
Year   **2005**

The artist Olaf Nicolai created this unique pack, which directly protects its contents and the safety of users, while indirectly protecting the natural environment through supporting the conservation of native Scottish woodlands (which have declined by 97 per cent since the late nineteenth century). Olaf worked with the Scottish government's forestry department to harvest a plantation of commercially grown Sitka spruce trees in Scotland's new national park, then turned them into matches that were packaged and sold to pay for the planting of native trees in the same location.

The pack is twice as long as a conventional matchbox, and contains huge matches that compel users to see, touch and smell the wood and the pink phosphor heads. The pink of the flame illustration – normally a warning symbol – matches the colour of, and makes a direct mental and visual connection with, the phosphor. As a result of the addition of red, yellow and purple, the flame seems to flicker and radiate signals that warn would-be users to be cautious.

More detailed information about the project is contained in a complementary postcard pack.

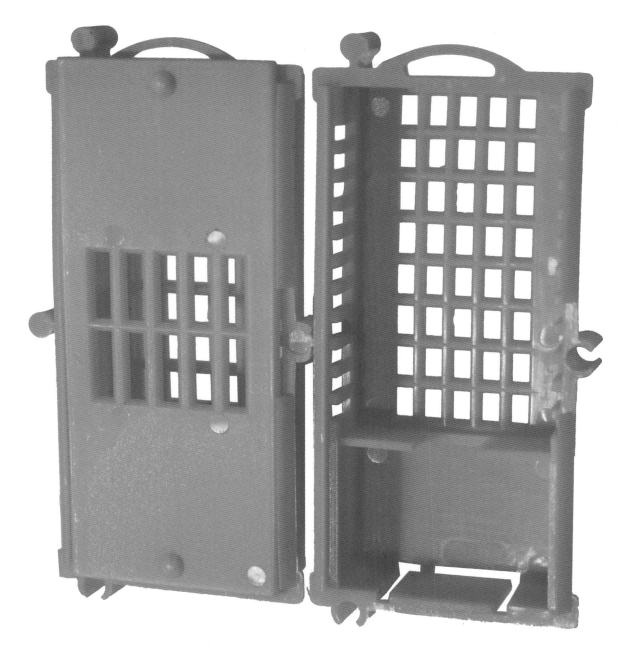

21

Pack	**Swienty Queen Bee Shipping Cage**
Client	**Swienty, Denmark**
Designer	**Bernhard Swienty, Denmark**
Year	**2001**

This cage demonstrates that protective packaging can be highly specialized, and includes keeping live animals safe when they are being transported. Honey bee queens are valuable, and are often taken to areas where they can revitalize ailing beehives and increase honey production and crop pollination.

The queen is put in a cage made from rigid plastic to prevent her being squashed or suffocated, as many cages are stacked tightly together to save space and transportation costs. Ventilation grilles keep her cool and allow her to be visually checked during transit. The queen's black and yellow colours contrast with the orange pack, making her easy to find.

The pack is designed to be placed in the hive where it continues to protect the queen by preventing her new colony of bees stinging her to death. The cage includes a candy-filled compartment, with a hinged door between the queen and the hive. As the queen slowly eats an escape route through the candy the bees familiarize themselves with her and accept her as their queen.

The packs are manufactured from a single injection-moulded polypropylene part that incorporates all the cage's closures, folds and hinges. They can be disinfected, and reused, or recycled.

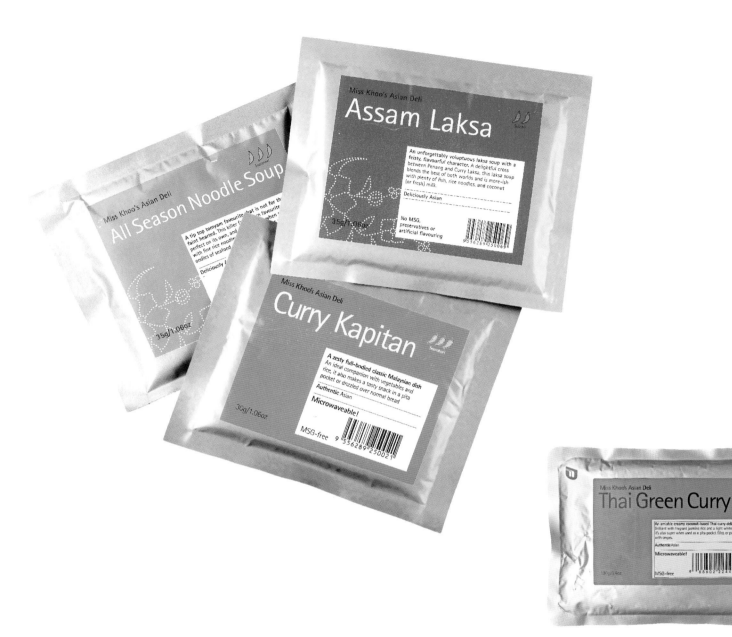

22

Pack   **Miss Khoo's Asian Deli food range**
Client   **Miss Khoo's Asian Deli, Malaysia**
Designer **Zerafina Idris and Fay Khoo, UK**
Year   **2000**

These unique packs protect the flavour of authentic Indian spices, modern Indian culture and the consumer's precious recreation time: each single-use sachet contains the ingredients and instructions required for a busy person to cook one gourmet, preservative-free Asian meal at home in less than ten minutes.

The full flavour of the spices is protected from the harmful effects of atmospheric gases and moisture by the use of commonly available microwave-friendly plastic and paper, plastic and foil, or composite vacuum-packing materials. The stylish grey and silver foils are also a shorthand way of communicating freshness and technology.

The minimalist approach to design capitalizes on the flat surfaces by using bright modern colours that evoke Indian culture and differentiate the products. It also delivers essential information quickly and clearly, with a common layout that helps consumers to compare the foods in the range. Product names are large with detailed descriptions printed legibly in black on white; instructions and other information are on the reverse of the pack. The outcome is a product that transcends traditional Asian food stereotypes by stripping away pseudo-cultural decoration and reducing the pack to its basic elements: sumptuous, expressive colours and beautifully crafted typography.

Pack   **Paperchase gift wrap**
Client   **Paperchase, UK**
Designer   **Paperchase, UK**
Year   **2007**

Paperchase sells designer stationery and printed gift-wrapping products whose monetary and cultural value is increased by the use of decorative outer packaging used to contain them. Its ever-changing range of decorative wrapping papers and associated tags, labels, boxes, bags, ribbons and trimmings is designed to enhance the status of a present and transform it into a special gift that celebrates a cultural event, birthday or holiday.

Value is also added to the company's associated generic products, including notebooks, greetings cards, boxes and files, by enveloping them in the same range of decorative patterns as the gift wrap. This allows them to be coordinated with other products.

The time invested in the process of selecting appropriate gift wrap and wrapping the gift has a worth that transcends monetary value and expresses the esteem in which the person who receives it is held. Skilful and sensitive packaging that demonstrates knowledge of the recipient is used to cement and protect relationships.

The process of unwrapping provides excitement and celebrates an occasion. It can be choreographed using multiple layers and different wrapping techniques. These are used to deliver suspense, drama, a gift that will be cherished and a memorable unwrapping experience.

Preserve

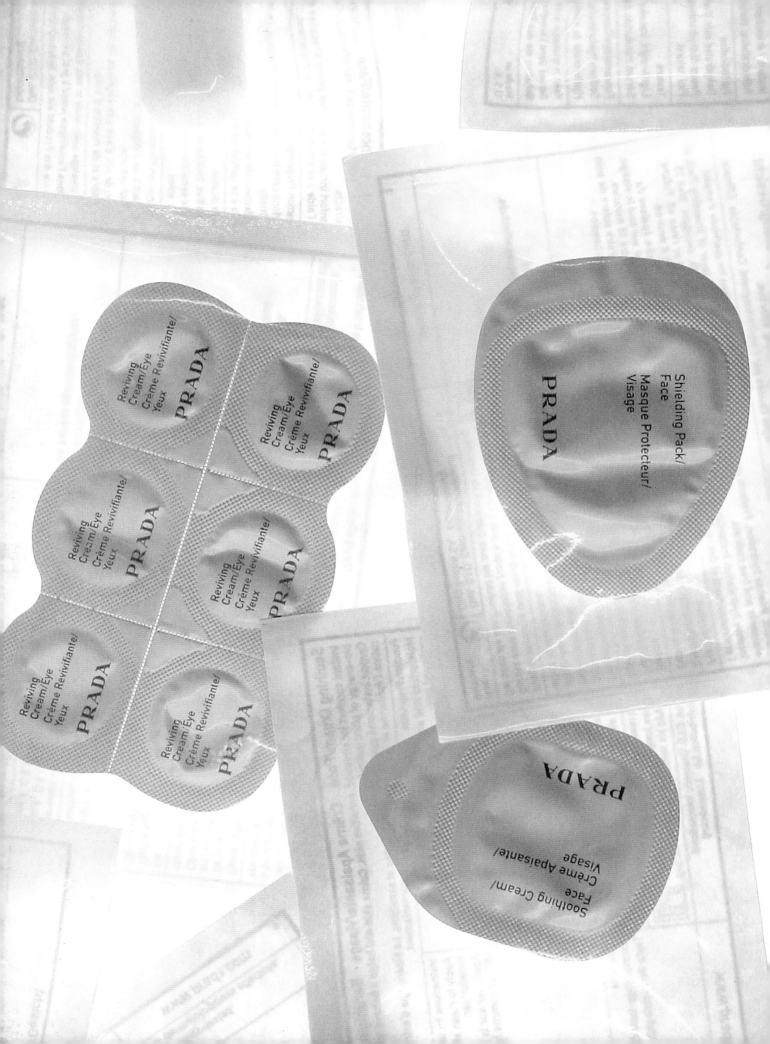

01   Prada cosmetics, by
Karim Rashid, USA, 2003. Prada's
cosmeceuticals merge packaging
traditions derived from both the cosmetics
and pharmaceuticals industries.

Overview
Packaging
that Preserves

Packs are often designed to prolong the life and integrity of their contents by excluding atmospheric gases, light, water, radioactivity, bacteria and even smells. Bags for supermarket salads are flushed with gases to inhibit the deterioration of roquette leaves and watercress, while others are designed to protect pharmaceuticals, face creams or seeds. The process of preservation is often extended to allow controlled removal of a product without jeopardizing the the rest of the pack and what it contains – an invaluable characteristic when dispensing precious commodities such as medicines, wine, cosmeceuticals and make-up, perfume and adhesives.

But while some packs are finessed to extend the shelf life or cupboard life of their contents, or to provide life support for living organisms, packaging has also evolved to preserve heritage, culture and tradition, and the integrity and longevity of brands.

Many of today's iconic packs have been around for over a century, and some for much longer. Gordon's® Gin was founded in 1769 and Fee Brothers Bitters in 1864. Ines Rosales, a relative newcomer, was established in 1910, while Orval has been brewing beer since around 1070 and Klaus Caramels making candy since 1856. Many packs have been with us, and our ancestors, for so long that they've become part of our personal histories and shared cultural 'wallpaper'. In this way our relationship with packaging is symbiotic – with packs becoming the props and backdrops in the drama of our everyday lives.

But packaging isn't just about people and their memories; it's also about places and their traditions. Packs play a vital role in the preservation of authentic regional specialities such as Andalusia's tortas, Kirriemuir's gingerbread and J&B Rare® Scotch Whisky. Some products, such as Camper shoes, Ortiz tuna, mackerel and anchovies and Toblerone chocolate, have extended their reach beyond their regional and national boundaries while others, like St Peter's Organic Ale and Traquair Jacobite Ale, remain closer to their sources, harder to obtain and arguably

higher in potential value; this makes them attractive precisely because they are rare and authentic, and ripe for exploitation.

Other packs reinforce regional differences. The variety of wrappings for the classic British 'fish 'n' chip' supper, and the many ways in which meat, flowers, hardware, cakes and bread are packaged, enrich – and are enriched by – local culture and traditions. Sadly, the humble paper bag, once a staple of every shop in every high street, is an endangered commodity that will hopefully be revived as an environmentally sustainable replacement for the polluting plastic bag.

After more than a hundred years of tinkering with the design of iconic packs, designers, manufacturers and investors now understand and value the heritage of ancient, culturally rich packaging that has been refined, distilled and proven over time. Heritage not only underpins and fertilizes brands; it also provides rich and lucrative material for their diversification into new sub-brands, product categories, sectors and geographical territories – and for many products, such as J&B Rare® Scotch whisky, the packaging is the major, most comprehensible and tangible part of a brand.

As a consequence, many global players have delved into their past with forensic fervour in order to remind themselves who they were and define who they now are, where they came from, and what makes them unique today and will continue to do so tomorrow. Some have invested in the creation of corporate archives – the drinks giant Diageo, for example, has established a museum-like depository of artefacts from the company's mercantile past, including items that range from signage and pub mirrors to Victorian point-of-sale and advertising. In today's world, preserving a brand-centred approach to the design of packs is just as important as maintaining the consistent visual appearance of a label. Even new products are made more valuable if they look old and designers find ingenious ways of investing packaging with synthetic heritage.

Just as brands become brands by being widely recognized, we learn to trust packs when they have been around for a while. Consistent appearance breeds familiarity, then trust, which short-circuits our decision-making and creates a direct route to our wallets. Put simply, businesses know that 'old' means 'gold'.

01   Camper Bolsa Pequeña carrier bag, by Martí Guixé, Spain, 2003. This quirky carrier bag protects and celebrates Camper's unique character.

02   Gordon's® Gin, by Diageo, UK, 2007. Gordon's signature logotype has subtly evolved since it first appeared around 250 years ago.

03   Chocovic Coberturas Selváticas, by Pati Núñez Associats, Spain, 2007. The exotic provenance of the cocoas used in these gourmet chocolate bars is expressed through Eva López's Rousseu-esque 'wild forest' illustrations.

04   Tunnock's Milk Chocolate Tea Cakes, by Archie Tunnock, UK, 2007. These iconic Scottish packs preserve a national tradition.

01

02

04

TARAKAN

75% cacao
chocolate negro

Selváticas
CHOCOVIC S.A. DESDE 1872

KENDARI

60% cacao
chocolate negro

Selváticas
CHOCOVIC S.A. DESDE 1872

NAYARIT

37% cacao
chocolate con leche

Selváticas
CHOCOVIC S.A. DESDE 1872

03

05   Kirriemuir Iced Gingerbread, by Bell Bakers, UK, 2007. The pack design of this regional cake has been preserved despite changing the substrate from paper to plastic.

06   Ortiz Bonito Frito, by Ortiz, Spain, 2004. Ortiz's canned fish help to preserve the history and traditions of the Basque fishing fleet.

07   J&B 1749®, by Diageo, UK, 1999. This glass bottle is based on an eighteenth-century wine flask and celebrates the 150th anniversary of the company's foundation.

08   Scottish Plain Loaf, by Marks & Spencer, UK, 2007. The utilitarian character of this traditional product is preserved by the extruded paper wrap and basic style of graphic design.

05

06

08

07

01   Fee Brothers Old
Fashion Aromatic Bitters. This
handmade scrunched-up paper
pack gives Fee Brothers' bottles
their unique, classic appearance.

02   The neck label celebrates four
generations of Fee Brothers' ancestry.

03   Detail of logo.

03

02

Case Study
Fee Brothers
Bitters

01

Pack	Fee Brothers Bitters
Client	Fee Brothers, USA
Designer	Fee Brothers, USA
Year	2007

This pack, originating from its first design in 1951, contrasts profoundly with other highly finished packs on the retail shelf and bar gantry because of its crumpled, unbleached paper wrapper and crazy confection of type styles, marks and colours.

The wrap-around paper label contains at least seven different typefaces in a mixture of capitals and lower case – centred, ranged, indented and expanded letterforms that are corralled and organized by an army of crude black keylines. Its surreal lozenge-shaped monogram is an unlikely amalgamation of type and numerals too bizarre, unpretentious and idiosyncratic to have been created by a professional designer.

The print quality is 'soft' and unfocused because the ink has bled into the unsurfaced paper as if it had been produced using old-fashioned printing and paper technologies. However, the sharpness of the smaller seriffed type confirms that the reproduction is modern and digital, and that the lozenge has simply softened by being endlessly copied so that its edges and sharp angles blurred and rounded before the label was eventually digitally scanned.

The neck label, printed in weird lime-green ink on sparkling white paper that clashes with the unbleached wrapper, illustrates a procession of moustache-wearing family members who resemble a Victorian barbershop chorus.

The overall effect is a pack whose detail convinces me that Fee Brothers is an idiosyncratic company that has remained true to its roots, through the Prohibition years of the 1920s and the Great Depression of the 1930s.

Modern designers find it almost impossible to overcome their high professional standards and create blurred type, mismatched papers or creased pack wrappers. In contrast to many cynical, polished, modern reinterpretations of old packs, this one has retained a genuine heritage that radiates history, confidence, pride and energy after all these years.

Interview with Joe Fee,
Treasurer and Sales Manager,
Fee Brothers

Is your pack deliberately designed to look old?
Well, that's just how it's always been done. I mean that it's 'hand done'. And, being the treasurer of the company, it gives me pain sometimes to see it – but it does have such value that I can get past my pain!

I think it's worthwhile to produce a pack that feels real and handcrafted rather than one that only has digital production values – which I think people can become immune to. I believe your product because it feels real, 'handmade' and personal. That gives it a higher value.
I always joke about our bitters being rolled on the thighs of an Italian virgin. There's a girl who does the job, and a lot of the labelling for us as well!

So, one person that does all this?
Well, no, not one person. But one person is very quick at it and she ends up doing it a lot of the time.

What's her name?
Delores.

01   Fee Brothers range of
cocktail flavourings retain many original
pack features developed since the
company's foundation in 1864.

01

Tell me about the history of the paper wrapper that covers the bottle.
Well, I think it was more a decision on my grandfather's part. My father did the neckband, to include the four Fee brothers.

Can you tell me how you would go about creating a new label?
Creating a new label? We kinda have our patterns set in terms of what we are doing… like a routine. Well, as an example, we just came out with a Grapefruit Bitters and so it was like, 'We are going to do a full wrap label, and a neck band on there, and what's the information we need on the Grapefruit Bitters?' There's a list of ingredients, our code and what have you, and so the format is pretty well set up.

How do you choose the label colour for each variety?
Well…ha ha! My sister and I grab our Pantone book and look at the colours we've already got. And we think about the fruit or the nut or whatever it is we are mimicking, and if the two of us agree on something we fly! It's not done by a panel or something like that.

What is the mark that sits within the diamond-shaped lozenge on the bottle – an 'FB' with two dots on it? Is it meant to be an illustration or is it a decorative monogram?
Purely a decorative monogram.

It's wonderfully unusual.
It is, and it just came out of my grandfather's head!

Do you have any plans to add your own face to the label?
The only way you can get your face on the label is either a) to grow a moustache. Or b) be dead! One I can't do and the other I am hoping to put off for a little bit!

02   Bottle label from the
range of bitters, which features
seven different typefaces.

02

Pack   **Hermanos Fernandez**
            butchery products
Client   **Hermanos Fernandez,**
            Spain
Designer   **Hermanos Fernandez,**
            Spain
Year   **2007**

Hermanos Fernandez is in the heart of Andalucian pig country, where the world's best ham, Pata Negra ('black hoof') is made, and has been making and selling traditional hams, chorizo, sausages and other pork products in the village of Galaroza for as long as anyone can remember. Over hundreds of years, traditions of wrapping and packaging have emerged that distinguish this part of Spain and preserve its reputation for artisan butchery.

In Andalucia, packaging is an extension of the butcher's trade and the routine of filleting, folding, extruding and tying – with string in the region's national colours of green and white. Wrapping and packing is a way of life that takes skill and time. It animates, and adds value to, commercial transactions by providing a space for conversation that cements the relationship between retailer and customer.

This kind of packaging has a grammar all of its own: cotton for ham, paper cones for raw meat, rolled paper for chorizo and air-dried sausage, wrapped paper for freshly made sausages – each method evolved to maintain the appropriate air and moisture content in the meat. The only big change in the last 50 years has been the addition of polythene carrier bags designed by selecting pictures, typefaces and colours from a printer's catalogue.

03

Pack   Camper 25th anniversary
              'Don't buy' and 'Pelotas'
              carrier bags
Client   Camper, Spain
Designer   Martí Guixé, Spain
Year   2002–3

Camper is an idiosyncratic shoe retailer that preserves its unique character through the design of its unconventional retail stores and its packaging design. Both have been created by the company in conjunction with Catalan artist, Martí Guixé, who has worked with Camper since 1997 to develop a conceptual approach to its business.

The printed paper bags are sized to contain a Camper shoe box and conceived to be portable physical and conceptual extensions of the company's shops that can be carried through the streets by the purchaser.

Pelotas is the name of a Camper shoe collection inspired by the design of old-fashioned soccer shoes. *Pelota* means 'ball',

such as a golf ball or football, and is a Basque ball game. The bag humorously celebrates the style of a Camper shoe, a traditional Basque game and '25 years of ball games'!

Guixé's 'Don't buy' carrier bag was designed as an ironic comment on retail consumption. It caught the imagination of the popular press and achieved cult status.

Preliminary drawings for the bags were undertaken on a computer using a pen tablet. However, the spontaneous and zany qualities of Guixé's early developmental sketches were preferred by the client because they suited the humorous Camper brand.

Pack   **Fuensanta limited edition water bottles**
Client   **Fuensanta, Spain**
Designer   **Pati Núñez Associats, Spain**
Year   **2008**

This limited edition pack was specifically designed to promote Fuensanta as a 'designer water' that would command a premium price in gourmet restaurants and shops.

Spare graphics and the simple, elegant shape of the bottle complement, and focus attention on, the pure clear water. The sophisticated and minimal 'silhouetted foliage' decoration evokes a natural product, and a beautiful forest of leaves is formed when bottles are grouped on a table or displayed in a shop. The simple typeface creates a balanced and carefully crafted composition that suggests care, skill and high value.

The lush valley of Fuensanta de Buyeres is in a national park in Asturias province on Spain's northwest coast. The area's medicinal springs, first recorded in 1270, were decreed a public utility by royal order in 1846, after which the therapeutic properties, flavour and mineralization of their water were widely enjoyed.

The 75 centilitre glass bottles are reusable and recyclable, and so help to preserve resources. The printed leaf silhouettes hint at the rich vegetation and wildlife that flourish in the region around the springs. Like the colour palette, the green metal enclosures suggest the company's 'green' attributes – Fuensanta supports environmental conservation and eco-efficiency in all its activities and is a founding patron of the local Asturias Bear Foundation, which preserves the wildlife of the region.

01   J&B Rare Scotch Whisky
packaging designed in 2007.
The bottle now has a sharper,
more modern silhouette.

02   J&B Rare Scotch Whisky
outer packaging designed around 1997.
The distinctive label design is applied
to outer cartons and other items
associated with the brand.

02

Case Study
J&B Rare®
Scotch Whisky

Pack   J&B Rare®
            Scotch Whisky
Client   Diageo, UK
Designer   Diageo, UK
Year   2007

While the whisky industry faces up to the challenge of not becoming an old man's drink, the bright and lively personality of J&B has successfully attracted young followers in over 130 countries, to become one of the world's largest whisky brands.

J&B's luminous attention-grabbing yellow label is highly visible on the bar, and its confetti of black and red letters confers upon it a glittering and complicated typographic honour that makes it appear distinguished, dynamic and thick with layers of history. While manufacturers may use this kind of typographic 'texture' to invest their packaging with fictional heritage, J&B Rare doesn't need to because Justerini & Brooks has supplied the royal households of many British monarchs.

Its yellow, red and black colours might hint that this drink should be approached with caution, respect and even reverence, but its historic green bottle – derived from the shape of a wine bottle – has undergone a profound re-design. The rounded silhouette has been sharpened, and the neck, shoulder and contour at the

bottom of the bottle made more angular. This creates an outline that is taut and twitchy with nervous energy and makes the pack look taller. These effects are heightened by the addition of a thick black, white and gold band around the perimeter of the label that emphasizes the pack's horizontal lines. Thickening the black and gold at the base of the label creates a heavy foundation that anchors the bottle on the shelf and gives it presence. These new horizontal elements work in parallel with reflections created by the sharpened glass contours, to deliver a controlled and intense composition that looks younger and, dare I say it, more aligned with other spirits – without diminishing its own.

Interview with Ewan Topping, J&B Global Communications Manager, and **Sabine van der Velden**, *Global Consumer Planning Manager, Diageo*

What is the story of J&B Rare?
ET: We are the 'unScotch Scotch' – that's something we say internally.

With the London address and 'St. James's' on the label and the royal patrons, J&B has a very London–Scottish feel about it.
ET: Actually Justerini and Brooks started off as wine and spirit merchants when an Italian gentleman came to the UK to follow an opera singer that he had designs on. That fell through but he decided to stay in London and set up a medicinal tonic wine business in 1749, and the original Justerini & Brooks company was founded. The original founders were George Adam Johnson and Giacomo Justerini, and the company was called Johnson & Justerini. In 1830, I think, it became Justerini & Brooks. They were official suppliers of fine wines and spirits to the royal household. They were producing 'Usige beatha', the Gaelic predecessor to whisky, as early as 1779. They first

01   J&B Rare Scotch Whisky packaging designed around 1997. J&B's unique attention-grabbing yellow and red label was probably based on the colours of London's Marylebone Cricket Club.

01

produced J&B Rare whisky for the post-Prohibition market in the United States. And, in terms of the pack, many of its cues came from the wine business – that's where the green bottle came from. It's unique among whisky bottles because wine, at that time, was bottled in green bottles and whisky was in clear bottles. It was a bold statement for the time and it really stands out. We are renowned but lively – and all those unique characteristics have helped us develop our 'party' brand. J&B has never been an armchair whisky. It has vibrancy and bold characteristics. As for the

actual graphic design of the label – one of the rumours is that the colours originated with the Marylebone Cricket Club.

Wow!
ET: We got some stuff out of history books that we found and I think – I'm not too sure about the exact details – that red and yellow were the colours of the club whisky. And then with J&B Rare, there was a fawn-coloured label for the American post-Prohibition market.

How do you brief designers to make incremental changes to the label? What would you not let designers mess with?
SV: There are things that we consistently keep, like the green bottle – that is who we are. The red and yellow on the label and also the size of the label, and the black letters on the label – that is what we call the 'jewellery'. We wouldn't be too keen on doing revolutionary things. We are an old brand and people are very protective about the label. We don't want to change this too much, but we still need to make sure it is relevant for today.

02 J&B Rare Scotch Whisky Mirrorball limited edition bottle. This version of the iconic pack was the focus of J&B's 'Start a Party' campaign to preserve the longevity of Europe's most popular Scotch by targeting it as a mixable party drink.

03 Detail of J&B Rare Scotch Whisky packaging designed in 2007. Lettering has been incorporated into the glass.

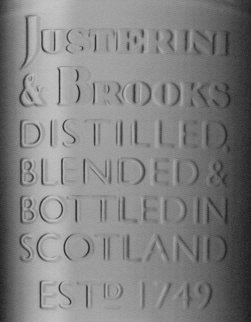

03

02

Are there variations in pack design between different countries and markets?
SV: No, not really.

You have really beautiful cartons that accompany the bottles – is there a range of other items that carry the design derived from the bottle label?
ET: None that we are currently producing, although there have been some examples. Generally sleeves (cartons) are a literal interpretation of the pack.

06

Pack　　　**Ines Rosales tortas**
Client　　**Ines Rosales, Spain**
Designer　**Juan Moreno, Spain**
Year　　　**2007**

These packs preserve the authentic look and feel of Ines Rosales' home-made Andalusian *tortas*, first produced in 1910.

Ines Rosales first sold her sweet, crunchy, aromatic biscuits, made with extra virgin olive oil, at the busy train station in Seville. She originally packaged them in a wooden box, lined with greaseproof paper to protect them from moisture and keep them crisp. Her packaging methods evolved over time to improve the crispness of the product and help keep consumers' hands free from olive oil.

By 1934 the biscuits were individually wrapped in greaseproof paper, and by the 1960s they were also available packed in sixes. In 1988 the business was sold and, in order to grow it, the new owner began the process of revitalizing the packaging.

The artisan qualities of these handmade biscuits are enshrined in these new packs, which preserve their heritage and secure their status as a niche regional product in the international marketplace. The use of translucent, single-colour, greaseproof-like paper maintains the pack's history and its unique style of hand-wrapping. The glossy sheen on the paper also expresses the appetizingly unctuous quality of the product.

07

Pack   Kirriemuir Gingerbread
Client   Bell Bakers, UK
Designer   Bell Bakers, UK
Year   2007

This picturesque package extends the shelf life of the cake it contains and reduces the need for preservatives. It also represents the culinary, literary and local history of a small town situated at the foot of the Grampian Mountains in Scotland.

Kirriemuir Gingerbread is a famous regional cake first produced over 80 years ago by a baker, Walter Burnett, in the Scottish town of Kirriemuir, and was originally packaged in a shiny, greaseproof wrapper. This new pack design retains the glossy appearance of the original but protects the cake by sealing in atmospheric gases and moisture that prevent it drying out. New plastics technologies mean that the substrate (polypropylene) currently used for the packaging will be replaced by environmentally sustainable alternatives such as PLA (polylactic acid), which is made from resins produced by fermenting starch and biodegrades in between six and 24 months.

The design on the front of the pack preserves the integrity of the original design and has only been incrementally altered over the last four decades. It features an illustration of a house and the caption, 'A window in Thrums'. The house is believed to be the birthplace of Sir James M. Barrie, author of *Peter Pan*.

08

Pack	**Klaus 1856**
	Caramels Tendres
Client	**Klaus, France**
Designer	**Claude Harry Barnardo,**
	France
Year	**2004**

This charmingly illustrated card outer pack for Caramels Tendres sweets commemorates the establishing in 1856 of Jacques Klaus's chocolate-making business in Switzerland.

One of the pioneering fathers of the Swiss chocolate industry, in 1903 Klaus founded the movement that helped consolidate the country's reputation as the world's centre of chocolate production. Since that time, beautifully illustrated 'chocolate box' packs have been used to promote the provenance and beneficial qualities of chocolate and sweets, thereby maintaining the integrity and longevity of brands such as Klaus for over 100 years. This romantic, childlike illustration depicts an idyllic Alpine scene complete with a strong farmer in national dress eating chocolate to keep him strong and healthy. In the background a cow reminds consumers of the creamy content, and texture, of caramel.

Klaus often used imaginary paintings to promote its products because consumers found them more compelling than photography. Illustrations have the advantage over photographs that they do not need to be realistic in order to communicate effectively. Illustration styles can also position a product in a precise time, place and context. For example, this image celebrates the Swiss confectionery tradition by portraying a golden past where eating traditional caramels was a good, simple, natural and wholesome milky pleasure.

09

Pack   **Orval Trappist Ale**
Client   **Brasserie D'Orval,
                Belgium**
Designer **Henri Vaes, Belgium**
Year   **2007**

Although the current brewery dates from 1931, the Cistercian monks of Orval in Belgium believe that beer was first brewed in their monastery in around 1070 – and the elegant silhouette of Orval's brown bottle and its idiosyncratic label demonstrate that packaging can simultaneously preserve more than one period in a product's history.

The off-white, black, gold and distinctive dusky mauve label and crimped metal enclosure contain the enigmatic illustration of a fish with a ring in its mouth that arouses the consumer's curiosity. The image, and the heraldic diamond-shaped lozenge refer to the legend of the monastery's foundation by Countess Mathilda of Tuscany in the eleventh century, when a trout allegedly retrieved her wedding ring from a fountain.

The whole pack, including its medieval remnants, is rendered in the Art Deco graphic style of the 1930s, which celebrates the foundation of the modern brewery and is now classic and never out of fashion. Amber is the traditional colour for beer bottles and contrasts pleasingly with the mauve label. It also preserves the product's stability and quality by protecting it against wavelengths of light that trigger 'skunking', a chemical reaction in hops that creates an offensive sulphurous aroma.

01 Ortiz fisherman catching white tuna. Cantabrian fishermen use traditional techniques, including rods and live bait, to catch White Tuna and preserve fish stocks.

02 Ortiz Bonito del Norte en Aceite de Oliva (White Tuna in Olive Oil). This unusual illustrated oval tin shows a modernized version of the company's original fishing boat design.

03 Ortiz Bonito Frito. The simple red, yellow, blue and silver colour palette contributes to this brand's distinctive appearance.

Case Study
Ortiz
canned fish

03

02

10

Pack   Ortiz canned fish
Client   Conservas Ortiz, Spain
Designer Conservas Ortiz, Spain
Year   2004

As the name of the company suggests, preservation is at the heart of everything Conservas Ortiz does.

The Ortiz fishing fleet is located on the coast of the Basque region of Spain where they fish for tuna, mackerel and anchovies in the Cantabrian Sea using traditional methods that sustain and preserve fish stocks.

Bonito del Norte on the can means 'Beauty of the North', and refers to the white tuna fish *Thunnus Alalunga*, which is caught by fishermen in open-topped boats using rods and live bait.

Another special product is anchovies. Once caught, they are filleted, boned and salted, and are arranged concentrically in wooden barrels and pressed under weights for six months. They are then washed and dried, and the amount of water and salt they contain is checked to ensure that the metal cans won't rust. The fillets are laid back to back in the cans, by hand – this arrangement, and the correct water content, makes sure the anchovies don't disintegrate on their journey to the customer. Ortiz describe their products as preserves or semi-preserves.

The preserves – tuna and mackerel – are packed in airtight containers, such as aluminium cans, and sterilized with heat to destroy potentially harmful micro-organisms that could contaminate them. They can be stored in perfect condition for many years and continue to undergo chemical changes that improve their flavour. Anchovies are classed as semi-preserves because they are salted rather than sterilized. They must therefore be stored in a cool environment to maintain their integrity.

Ortiz's brightly coloured cans feature a new version of their original fishing boat design, which is printed directly on the cans rather than being on a card outer carton. This reduces the amount of material used, and capitalizes on the attractive oval and round cans that express the brand's heritage. The predominance of yellow – the most luminous colour in the spectrum – makes the products highly visible on the retail shelf and too attractive to hide in the kitchen cupboard.

Interview with Jacobo Múgica, Export Manager, Conservas Ortiz

Who designed these iconic packs? The packs were originally designed in the 1930s by an unknown Catalan designer. The design was engraved in limestone, and the original form of lithography, which takes its name from the Greek word *lithos* meaning 'stone', was used to print it. Since then, lots of modifications have been undertaken to promote the traditional and unique aspects of the products.

Moreover, the brand's three principal sources of inspiration are presented on the packs. The blue fringe of waves is reminiscent of the sea, and the cans are illustrated with a traditional fishing boat that is being pushed by fishermen. Our modern cans are made of aluminium rather than tinplate and are easy to open. They are also recyclable and have less impact on the environment than plastic. However, along the way Ortiz has done everything possible to maintain the 'soul' of the original design.

01   Serie Oro Exquisitos Filetes
de Anchoas. The golden colour palette
and additional decoration used on
this tin expresses the supreme quality
of traditional craftsmanship used
in the preparation of this particular
species of gourmet anchovy.

01

*How long did it take to
develop the new packs?*
We don't know how long
it took to develop the first
ones, but they are being
constantly evolved because
we will never stop trying
to improve their design.

*How many people have
worked on this project?*
Many people have worked on
it because it began back in the
1930s, and since then various
design agencies have gradually
evolved the design of the packs.

*How many prototype versions
do you make?*
We honestly don't know, but
the important thing is that
the project has changed a lot
and many different prototypes
have been developed at each
stage of the process. But at
all stages of improving the
packs numerous packaging
tests have been done, with our
customers and with our clients.

*Were there any difficult problems
you had to overcome?*
The biggest difficulty is
improving a pack without
destroying its soul and its
essential character. Today,

maintaining the Conservas
Ortiz image is quite difficult.
Selling quality in a can is also
complicated, because cans have
historically been associated with
the mass market, as low-quality
food or produce that is not
fresh. Our packs have to sell
tradition and quality, but they
also have to follow the evolution
of society and technology.
That is our main aim.

*Would you have done
anything differently?*
We have been working on
many packaging projects
centred around these cans and
all of them have failed. For

02   Verdel Frito Escabechado.
This tin plays the visual trick of
showing its contents – fried mackerel
in local Escabeshado sauce.

03   Family Reserve Anchovies.
Contemporary illustrations of Basque
crafts help to preserve regional traditions.

04   Ortiz Ventresca de Bonito del
Norte en Aceite de Oliva. This gourmet
product contains only the most delicate
part of the fish. Its superior quality is
signified by an additional outer pack.

04

03

02

example, we tried to change
the logotype and the colours,
and it didn't work. We do
have to continue with the
incremental modifications that
improve the packs, but they
should not be huge changes.

*What is your next packaging
project?*
We are working on many
projects including a new range
referred to as 'prepared plates',
called 'Reserva de Familia' or
'Special Selection of the Family'.
Each year the packs change,
like the *costera* (fishing season).

11

Pack   Rare Malts Selection
              Caol Ila® Aged 23 Years
Client   Diageo, UK
Designer   Sedley Place, UK
Year   2002

With its sensitive and sophisticated reinterpretation of the traditional whisky bottle, this fastidiously designed pack preserves the essence of rare and expensive single cask-strength malt whisky.

The unembellished pewter-coloured metal enclosure is a subtle historical reference, and tells connoisseur consumers that the designer, and the producer, understand the true nature and value of this premium drink.

Typography is a key element in communicating the subtle differences in origin, age, cask strength, dates and registered numbers. In order to heighten the importance of this information there are two labels placed on the bottle with self-conscious precision; the whisky is an exacting product made by precise methods for a niche market that is characterized by its ability to detect nuance, and value products accordingly.

A generic blue and gold label describes the context and is composed in a nostalgic Victorian style with chamfered edges. A white, black and red label contains product-specific information and is designed in a utilitarian 1940s style with rounded corners. The labels combine to express the nineteenth-century foundations of the distilleries. If you partially close your eyes you can see how the labels yield their information in descending order of importance.

12

Pack　　Selfset Rat Trap
Client　Selfset, UK (a division
　　　　of Falcon Works, UK)
Designer　Selfset, UK
Year　　2007

This sturdy card box with RAT emblazoned in vertical capital letters acknowledges our fear of an ancient pest by shouting its name and capturing our attention. It stands out like a medieval anachronism on a modern retail shelf.

The carton preserves, and connects purchasers with, history by stylistically celebrating the sanitary crusade that reached its zenith in the late nineteenth and early twentieth centuries. Based on an original design dating from 1947, its hand-drawn type technologically mirrors the lo-tech trap, reassuring the consumer that old-fashioned, tried and tested mechanical science works, and has even been improved ('New principle release action') for today's modern world. 'No trapped fingers' stimulates the imagination and neatly conveys the efficacy of the device.

The manufacturer of this sinister killing machine told me a darkly humorous story that is too good not to include here: 'The packs were originally packaged by hand, but some time ago orders were running behind and it was decided to send thousands of traps to be packaged by the inmates of a hospital for the criminally insane. The inmates made up the traps, but one of them set them and put them in the box, so they were ready to go off as soon as the box was opened. Fifteen thousand traps had to be recalled, disarmed and repackaged.'

13

Pack   **Prada cosmetics**
Client   **Prada, Italy**
Designer **Karim Rashid, USA**
Year   **2003**

These unique packs exploit the hygiene and convenience of pharmaceutical 'blister' packs. Made from plastic and aluminium foil, they are designed to deliver measured quantities of skincare products.

Each single blister is peeled and squeezed to obtain its contents, and is then discarded. This prevents users making the expensive mistake of applying excessive amounts of the product. Single-dose packaging also enhances the cosmetic's perceived potency and its high value.

The utilitarian drugstore blister packs are softened and feminized by the addition of curvaceous, softly sculpted dye-cut edges before they are heat-sealed within translucent petal-coloured polythene envelopes. The Prada logotype clearly marks the packs as containing products that are both 'premium' and 'potent' – a combination of high fashion and science. The overall effect is of a distinctive and innovative skincare language and experience.

Single-dose dispensing also ensures that the cosmetics are 'fresh' and untainted by the effects of the environment, unlike those in larger volume packs, which are exposed time after time through daily use. Theoretically, this means that the products require fewer additives and preservatives and are, indeed, 'fresher' than their competitors in larger packs.

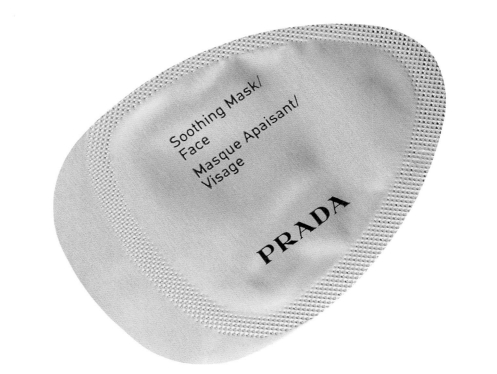

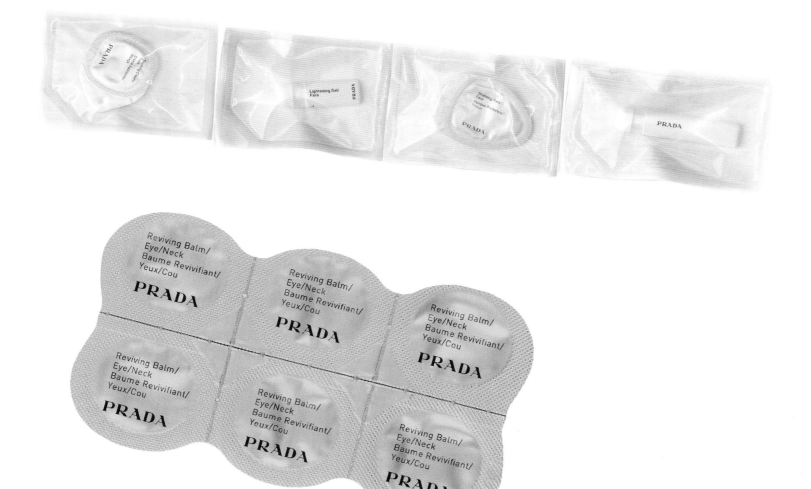

Well, no one can quite put their finger on it. "Cola with an edge" is what the hardcore cola geeks who taste-tested and loved it said. The other special thing about Ubuntu is that it is the first – and only – cola in the UK to get the Fairtrade stamp of approval. Try one and see how you feel.

ubuntu – a new kind of cola.

www.ubuntu-trading.com

01　　　Ubuntu Cola advertisement.
Ubuntu Cola's packaging contrasts with
its much larger red-coloured competitors
by being white, calm and fizzy.

02　　　Ubuntu Cola on the retail
shelf. The cans form an attractive
effervescent pattern of bubbles
when displayed together.

02

Case Study
Ubuntu Cola

14

Pack　　　Ubuntu Cola
Client　　Ubuntu Trading
　　　　　Company,
　　　　　South Africa
Designer　Simon Porteous, UK
Year　　　2007

Ubuntu Cola epitomizes the evolution of new ethical businesses that participate in the fairtrade movement, which works to empower small farmers in Africa and other developing countries that export products such as coffee, soya and sugar.

Ubuntu translates as 'humanity' and 'kindness', and means 'I am what I am because of who we all are'. It describes the 'give and take' concept of sharing and mutual dependency that is the ethos of the Ubuntu Trading Company.

Ubuntu's founder, Sandy Muir, identified the opportunity for an ethical cola after discovering that caffeine was a by-product of fairtrade decaffeinated coffee. When mixed with fairtrade sugar and other ingredients it would create an alternative to big brand colas. However, branding and packaging were crucial in delivering a product that could compete in the world's most iconic consumer market.

The cola was therefore packed in a standard recyclable aluminium can made by Rexam, who also manufacture packaging for Coca-Cola and Pepsi. This moves it away from fairtrade's association with less branded primary commodities such as tea, coffee and sugar into the sophisticated branded marketplace in which it competes.

The simple graphic design of Ubuntu's pack differentiates it from its monolithic competitors, and from the predominantly red-coloured supermarket 'own brand' colas. The design also metaphorically describes the journey from the direct and undecorated style of the black and white, sans serif Ubuntu logotype, through bubbles to the Fairtrade Foundation's endorsement. The bubbles, and their size and relationship with each other, are metaphors for Ubuntu's ideology of interdependent communities, ideologies and aims. The unpretentious pattern, bright colours and sparkling white background suggest a straightforward relationship between grower and consumer, and are light, optimistic and modern.

Interview with Miranda Walker,
Managing Director, Ubuntu
Trading Company

Who is Ubuntu marketed to?
The target market is people aged 20 to 30, who like to feel that they're making a contribution and that there is an ethical element to their purchases. They include students from second year upwards, young professionals and the 'Waitrose shopper'. Ubuntu is consumed in the company of others, so they have the feeling of being at one with other people. We're very keen that it should be an attractive brand that has social credibility.

Are other cola manufacturers interested in Ubuntu Cola?
We've not had a response from any of our competitors. We 'soft launched' because we're a niche brand and we're small – we're not setting out to take on the big boys. What we see is a very big market, worth around £3.8 billion [$4.5 billion] in the UK, where there ought to be a fairtrade option. We have had a lot of interest from abroad and we are now exporting to Scandinavia and also Ireland.

01   Ubuntu Cola development
visual showing the bubbles and
Fairtrade endorsement emerging as
key elements of the final pack design.

01

Why did you produce a white pack?
We looked at a broad spectrum
of designs because we wanted
something that expressed the
Ubuntu idea, and we wanted
to attract young people. At
one end of the spectrum we
looked at quite hardcore,
funky designs. Those had great
teenage appeal but didn't have
fairtrade cues. At the other
end of the spectrum we looked
at beautiful, ethnic, African
'authentic' designs which the
fairtrade supporters loved,
but they didn't want to drink
cola out of them – they wanted
an organic elderflower juice
to come out of the can. I was

concerned about African cues
– although our proposition is
absolutely about supporting
Africa – because a pack that
looked as though it was made
in Africa wouldn't have the
'quality' cues that we were
trying to achieve, and, worse
than that, there was a danger
of it appearing patronizing.
          We looked at a wide
range of colours and came
to the white very quickly. We
moved away from red almost
instantly because if you have
too much red you look like a
'me too' coke and are straight
into supermarket 'own label'
territory. You need a little bit

of red on the pack in order
to signify 'cola' – that's
absolutely the colour that's
associated with cola – but if
you let the red dominate
you look like a cheap 'me
too' brand.
          The white we loved
for its stand-out. We loved it
because of the all the semiotic
associations of the colour –
of goodness, simplicity and
purity, and purity of intention
in the Ubuntu idea. And then
we came to it quite quickly.
It's a nightmare to work with
because it shows up absolutely
everything, and it's very
difficult to get a good white

02   Ubuntu Cola pack. The
Fairtrade logotype is a key ingredient of the
Ubuntu Cola brand and therefore occupies
a prominent position on the front of the
pack. The bubble pattern also abstractly
describes the ethos of 'interdependence'
that underpins Ubuntu's brand.

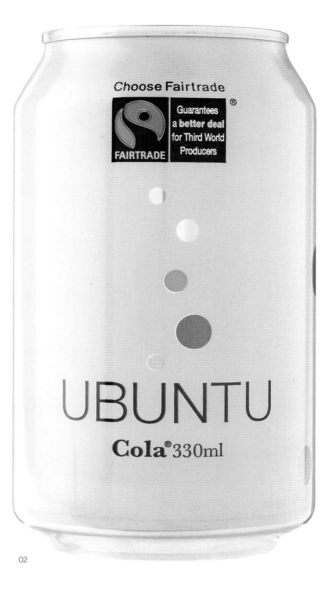

02

printed on a can, but we're
very pleased we went with it.
          We also love the
bubbles. And we wanted
bubbles rather than an
obvious interpretation of
'interdependence' which
would be links in a chain or
people shaking hands. We
wanted something that was a
more abstract interpretation.

15

Pack   **Traquair Jacobite Ale**
Client   **Traquair House, UK**
Designer **Brian Ford/**
         HGV Design, UK

Year   **2007**

This diminutive bottle is exceptional. Its unusual size and sleek monochrome appearance betray its potency and cultural history, while its vernacular label, drawn by artist Brian Ford, alludes to the family and regional traditions that the ale embodies.

The glossy black-brown bottle is the traditional, and almost forgotten, way of packaging Scottish ales. The dark colour and crimped metal enclosure prevent light and atmospheric gases tainting the ale and convey its authentic origins – the brewery was established in twelfth-century Traquair House at Innerleithen, in Scotland, in the eighteenth century. Its handcrafted and hand-applied paper label depicts Bonnie Prince Charlie (Charles Edward Stuart), an image copied from a rare eighteenth-century Jacobite drinking glass owned by Traquair House.

The ale was launched in 1995 to commemorate the 250th anniversary of the 1745 Jacobite uprising, when the prince came to Traquair to ask the earl to support him in his campaign to retake the British throne for the Stuarts. The earl promised him that the gates of Traquair would not be opened until this objective had been achieved. The gates remain closed to this day and are featured on the bottle's reverse label.

Jacobite Ale was originally intended to be a 'limited edition'. However, because of its success, which is partly due to the packaging, production continues and sales have increased.

16

Pack   **Trotter Gear**
             Unctuous Potential
Client   **St. John, UK**
Designer   **Fergus Henderson**
             and Annabel Harty, UK
Year   **2007**

Fergus Henderson is head chef at the St. John restaurant in London, where he promotes 'nose to tail eating' – using every part of an animal. His signature style of simple British cooking using offal and traditional seasonal ingredients has made him a unique figure on the international culinary stage.

Unctuous Potential is Trotter Gear's (and Fergus's) first packaged product: jellied pig's trotter. A straightforward vacuum-packed polythene bag is used to extend its shelf life and make it appear authentic and home-made. Simple single-colour graphics are printed on card, which is attached to the plastic with an old-fashioned rivet. The pack also features Fergus's own style of language which is funky, lyrical and eccentric in a peculiarly English way: '... comprises nudgels of giving wobbly pig's trotter captured in a splendid jelly... adds "wobbly magic" to meat dishes and stews'. This rhetorical style expresses Fergus's character and communicates the culinary heritage behind the product.

The black-and-white image of a pig is St. John's trademark: a nineteenth-century engraving of a butcher's diagram showing a pig's carcass with a compliant, smiling face. This, and the funky name, give the pack a hip, quaint and distinctively whimsical character.

17

Pack   **Tunnock's Milk**
           Chocolate Tea Cakes
Client   **Thomas Tunnock, UK**
Designer **Archie Tunnock,**
           Thomas Tunnock, UK
Year   **2007**

These packs survive because they have preserved their essential character for nearly half a century. Founded in 1890, Tunnock's first produced teacakes in the 1950s; they soon became popular and now sell in 30 countries.

Based on a design originally dating from the 1960s, the teacakes themselves look refreshingly uncontrived in today's cynical commercial world where it can be difficult to distinguish genuine history from fake. Their simple cartoon-cake shapes, childlike shiny, striped aluminium foil wrappers and colourful point-of-sale boxes endure because of the product's 'natural' recipe and because the pack designs do many things well.

The cheerful card box has a bright yellow background that is luminous and stands out on the shelf. The rosy-cheeked child, and other optimistic, naive illustrations with wonky perspectives, jolly type and simple commercial banners (shapes containing type), create the impression of a thoroughly honest product that is a welcome anachronism compared with its modern, commercially savvy competitors.

The language used on the packs evokes the unabashed goodness of the 1950s, when consumers and manufacturers trusted each other and people bought things simply because they were good. Words like 'finest' and 'pride' are endearingly guileless, and persuade us that Tunnock's is as proud of its products as it is of their now cool and very fashionable Scottish roots.

18

Pack   **VAT 69® Blended Scotch Whisky**
Client   **Diageo, UK**
Designer **Diageo, UK**
Year   **2003**

The menacing design of the VAT 69 bottle makes this Scotch whisky different from the other 2,500 brands currently marketed. It uniquely preserves the essential character of Scotch as it used to be perceived – as an often illegal, and sometimes dangerous, 'man's' drink. This is both an unsettling reminder of its potency and a welcome relief from the many other, more civilized and decoratively refined Scotch whisky packs that promote a romantic history rather than a historically correct, if unfashionable, version of the past.

The very name VAT 69 suggests a whisky barrel or dark green glass bottle within which, like George Orwell's Room 101, a sinister potential lurks. The dour rectangular black label with its big, white, stencilled type bawls VAT 69 with a warning flash of yellow banding. The unbalanced angle of the name is less a reminder of the text on a wooden whisky barrel, which is its true heritage, and more a warning that a terrible force has been unleashed, spreading the ink with the force of its impact.

VAT 69's biggest export markets are Venezuela, Spain and Australia – countries perhaps known for their overtly masculine cultures. The whisky was also Sir Ernest Shackleton's companion on his harrowing Imperial Trans-Antarctic Expedition of 1914 – confirming its status as the Scotch of heroes.

19

Pack	**Wallace Land o' Cakes paper bag**
Client	**Wallace Family Bakers, UK**
Designer	**Andrew Wallace, UK**
Year	**1996**

Paper bags illustrate and describe the unique catalogue of shops that once lined our high streets and help to preserve our cultural heritage. They were also a conduit for, and the reason behind, rare commercial typefaces and sustained many local printing businesses. Their demise has left a historical and sensorial vacuum that cannot be filled by the ingress of chain stores and their polythene carrier bags. Plastic does not deliver the satisfying feel, smell and crinkling sound of a crisp paper bag, which simultaneously communicates the qualities of 'newness' and 'freshness'.

Five generations of the Wallace family have been bakers in the city of Dundee in Scotland.

At one point in the company's history there were seven brothers, each with his own bakery. In 1926 Andrew Wallace commissioned a bag design for the bakeries that featured the Wallace monument, an iconic local landmark that celebrates the hero whose name the bakers shared: William Wallace, leader of the Scottish resistance to the English in the thirteenth century. 'Land o' Cakes' is a reference to Robert Burns's colourful culinary description of Scotland.

This simple paper pack preserves heritage on many different levels, and is an effective and environmentally sustainable alternative to polythene packaging.

20

Pack   Paxton & Whitfield
            paper bag
Client   Paxton & Whitfield, UK
Designer   Stratton Windett, UK
Year   2003

This straightforward pack demonstrates the unique way in which the excellence of products and services can be formally recognized by the Queen and members of the royal family, including the Duke of Edinburgh and the Prince of Wales. This automatically connects companies with a heritage and tradition that dates back to medieval times. The granting of a royal warrant instantly adds prestige and monetary value to goods.

Since the fifteenth century the royal chamberlain, on behalf of the royal household, has issued tradesmen with warrants of appointment to supply the court with high-quality goods and services. Today, they are granted to companies and individuals for periods of up to five years. During this time a business is permitted to display the royal arms and the words 'By Appointment' on its packaging, stationery, vehicles and buildings, and use them in advertisements.

Paxton & Whitfield has an impressive total of seven warrants for supplying cheese to the royal household, including two that are current today. The use of the associated heraldic endorsements on its paper bags proves that a medieval system of communication has evolved to become an effective modern method of graphically expressing quality.

21

Pack   **St Peter's Organic Ale**
Client   **St Peter's Brewery, UK**
Designer **St Peter's Brewery, UK**
Year   **2007**

This special bottle shows how preserving something genuinely old can simultaneously create an unexpectedly modern-looking pack design.

When John Murphy, chairman of St Peter's Brewery, found a bottle in his attic he copied it exactly to create the distinctive one used by the brewery. He then discovered that the original bottle was produced for Thomas Gerrard, an innkeeper on the Delaware River in Gibbstown, Philadelphia, and dates from around 1770. St Peter's logotype was also designed by John Murphy, and depicts a raven and a key in a barrel. The brewery is in St Peter's Hall in Suffolk, an ancient building with a half-moat.

Historically, moats provided protection against maurauders and became status symbols. The raven similarly signifies status, prestige and protection, while the key represents the 'key to heaven', which is said to be held by St Peter.

The pack's bold silhouette, small label and uncluttered retail face are designed to showcase the beer inside. Wavy lines cast into the glass hide any sediment that might settle on the bottom of the bottle, while the oval section, similar to the exhaust pipe of an expensive car, makes the pack more comfortable to hold than the more common round bottle, and immediately distinguishes it from competitors.

22

Pack   **Toblerone**
Client   **Kraft Foods, USA**
Designer   **Kraft Foods, USA**
Year   **2007**

Theodor Tobler created Toblerone's famous name in 1908 by combining Tobler with *torrone*, the Italian word for nougat. By taking his inspiration for the bar's triangular shape from Switzerland's mountains, he also created an affordable national icon that sells in over 122 countries, in seven different flavours.

Over the years the pack design and its distinctive typography, colours and trademarks have been refined to preserve the product's family roots and Swiss cultural heritage. The now familiar mountain image once contained a bear to represent its founder's birthplace, the city of Berne. This replaced an eagle that was depicted carrying a

flag with the letter 'T'. The old-fashioned commercial typeface, originally in the Art Nouveau style fashionable in Tobler's era, has been modernized. Today the letters are more uniformly and symmetrically composed, but still look authentically old.

The rich blue drop shadow is more colourful and vibrant than the previous black one. This creates an illusion of depth which, along with the original chamois background, helps the pack to stand out on the shelf. It also emphasizes the product's high production values, and therefore its high quality. This is reinforced by the pleasing texture of the shallow embossing.

Perform

MARKS &
SPENCER

biological
laundry powder

- contains cleaning ingredients derived from plant sources**
- contains natural fragrance
- contains no colours
- contains no phosphates
- effective even at 30° C

1kg e

10
STANDARD
WASHES*

80%
RECYCLED
PAPER

CARTON

01   Biological Laundry Powder,
by Marks & Spencer, UK, 2007.
This pack performs by seamlessly
extending the design and colour
of product into the pack.

Overview
Packaging
that Performs

All packs perform to a greater or lesser extent, but the packaging in this section performs in four very specific ways.

Firstly, some packs are designed to be deformed and effectively destroyed in controlled ways by consumers, in order to yield their contents. Dylon Cold Water and Multipurpose Dyes must be stabbed and punctured before they can be used. Others involve less dramatic and violent interference: the Fungi Foray condiment pack is gently shaken, while matches are struck, and chocolate bars are ripped open and their contents broken and devoured. All of these different kinds of packaging require us to play a dynamic role in their destruction in order to release their contents and conclude the performance. However, in addition to the superficial drama, a lot is happening behind the scenes.

These different unwrapping processes perform by creating rituals – cultural by-products that prolong the enjoyment of the unwrapping experience and add additional value to the product. Some of these rituals are embedded in tradition, while others are invented and encouraged by manufacturers. For artists, uncapping Winsor & Newton's talismanic little tubes of watercolour paint, then squeezing the contents on to the palette, is a familiar and reassuring routine that's rooted in history but also calms the mind before the creative action. Rituals can be soothing and enjoyable and are therefore a powerful way of creating lucrative and long-term relationships between consumers and products.

Hazel Selina's Ecopod coffin is destroyed in a slightly different way. It is specifically designed to be the focus of the cultural performance that's organized around it. Decoration, and apparently expensive materials such as gold and silver leaf, add drama to the ceremony of death and burial, and transform a simple paper casket into a complex and valuable object, which is itself transformed as it decomposes in the ground or is burned in the crematorium in an ecologically-friendly way – which leads me to the second way in which packs can perform.

A growing number of packs are designed not to harm the environment, and achieve this objective in different ways. These include being made from recycled and recyclable materials that can be reused or will biodegrade in the compost heap. Or packs can simply use less material so that fewer harmful carbon emissions are created during their manufacture and distribution. Governments exert pressures on businesses to reduce the environmental impact of their operations. This means that many companies like IKEA take a holistic view of their activities and work to reduce the impact of their packaging at every stage of its lifecycle, including during its manufacture, distribution and afterlife. Businesses are also aware of the increasing pressure exerted upon them by customers who are demanding fewer wasteful packs and more recyclable and compostable solutions. This challenges designers and manufacturers to make packs that use less energy and materials which leads to the creation of new materials, and printing and other production processes, that are environmentally friendly.

Thirdly, packs perform by adding value. The composition and decoration of the materials used to contain a product can change how it is perceived in the same way that water in a crystal glass is seen to have a higher value than water in a disposable plastic cup.

Designers sometimes have difficulty in objectively and intelligently deconstructing, analyzing, understanding and controlling the many different ways in which packs perform. Quality is often most evident in the details – in the juxtaposition of materials or in finely-crafted type – as seen in the design approach used to create Molton Brown's and Woolrich's packs. Using fewer elements in a design often means it is more highly valued than a conspicuously over-decorated pack. However, simplicity demands higher levels of skill and control from the designer and a consumer who is able to appreciate the craftsmanship. Thankfully both can be achieved through education and practise and good examples abound – look no further than Apple, Comme des Garçons or Marks & Spencer.

Fourthly, the way packs perform dynamically and ergonomically can have a big effect on how we interact with, and regard, them. The click of a lid being securely shut reassures us in the same way that the hiss of gas when a can of Guinness® Draught is opened makes the taste buds tingle in anticipation of a perfectly poured drink. Packaging is a total performer and a feast for all of the senses, not just for the eyes.

01   Basi Homme & Basi Femme, by Pati Núñez Associats, Spain, 2007. The round-edged shapes of these bottles were inspired by the eroded forms of sea-washed pebbles to create forms that beg to be touched and used.

02   Scottish Bluebell matches, by ccb, Sweden, 2008. This pack of safety matches may be made, or derived, from wood but they are more environmentally sustainable than plastic disposable lighters.

03   IKEA SMAL 12 x drink stirrers. This pack performs by doing more with less and revealing the attractive, bright colours of the product.

04   Fungi Foray Shake O' Cini, by Ken Reilly, UK, 2000. This decorative fungi container also performs as a condiment shaker.

01

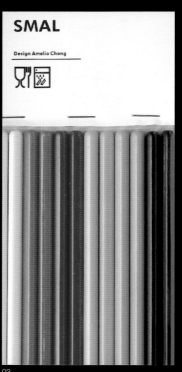

03

04

02

05   Chocolate,
by Rohr, Switzerland, 2007.
These chocolates perform as
edible packages and include a
luscious chocolate logotype.

06   Alcor, by Pati Núñez
Associats, Spain, 2006. This wine label
performs by alluding to the story of the
wine's creation, after a night of stargazing.

07   Comme des Garçons
Series 5: Sherbet, by Rei Kawakubo,
Japan, 2000. Fragrance packaging
works hard to dramatize the particular
character of its contents. These pale
pastel- coloured packs express the
soft sugary fruit flavours of sherbet.

08   Artists' Water Colour,
by Winsor & Newton, USA, 2007.
These interactive packs perform by
expelling paint when squeezed.

09   Cold Water Dye, by Dylon,
UK, 2007. These little tins must be
stabbed and punctured before
they will perform.

05

06

08

09

07

01   BP Gas Light 5kg (11lb) pack. The design has changed the appearance of this pack from that of a crude industrial bomb to a translucent bottle of fuel that reassures consumers by revealing its contents.

02   BP Gas Light 5kg (11lb) and 10kg (22lb) packs. Lightweight materials mean Gas Light is easier to carry than metal canisters.

Case Study
BP LPG
Gas Light

02

01

Pack	BP LPG Gas Light
Client	BP LPG, UK
Designer	Ragasco, Norway
Year	2000

This innovative lightweight liquified petroleum gas (LPG) pack is revolutionizing the domestic gas-bottle market for consumers who use it to power items such as barbecues and caravan stoves.

Insights from BP's customer research revealed that gas bottle users found steel bottles increasingly difficult to handle; they were too heavy, rusty and you never knew how much gas you had left. However, the design of this new pack has defused and domesticated the way in which flammable gas is packaged, and even manages to reassure the customer by being user friendly.

BP Gas Light delivers many innovations, including safety features that mean the pack will not corrode and leak flammable gas, or explode and scatter potentially lethal metal shrapnel if there's a fire. The new packs are also half the weight of standard steel bottles, acknowledging that many users felt that the steel bottles are just far too heavy to lift. BP Gas Light is translucent, so consumers can check the product level to ensure they do not run out of gas unexpectedly.

The vast majority of the pack is fully recyclable and reusable, and its corrosion-proof fibreglass casing, sporty moulded plastic handle-cum-valve-protector, leaf-patterned outer casing, and green and white colour scheme express qualities including 'outdoor sport', 'leisure' and 'nature' rather than a 'crude industrial gas cylinder'. This is vital in a market where customers want safe, portable energy that also performs as a stylish accessory for their expensive barbecues or trailer.

By using packaging to add value to a utilitarian product and make it safer, easier and more attractive, BP has been able to move it up the value chain. The results speak for themselves. Around 50 per cent of sales come from new users of LPG appliances, many of whom are attracted by the new style bottle.

Interview with Craig Stoddart,
Marketing Development
Manager, BP LPG

Did you know there was a gap in the market?
Yes, and the feedback we were getting from customers was that gas bottles were heavy, dirty, rusty and difficult to handle … and that you would never know when you ran out of gas.

Did you pilot the bottle?
Around 2000 or so we found a company in Norway (Ragasco AS) that was developing the technology – and a lightweight and translucent bottle. We took the bottle from them as one of their early customers, having clearly seen the benefits it could have to our own customers.

People spent £200 or £300 [$300 to $400] on a nice barbecue and then we found that they were buying little jackets to cover the steel bottle. That told us that people wanted something nice on their patios.

How did you develop the decorative aspects of the bottle?
The inside is a blow-moulded plastic liner that holds the gas. The strength of the bottle comes from what is wrapped

01   BP Gas Light detail of valve
and neck. The handles also perform
as a protector for the metal valve.

01

around that liner – it's composite fibreglass and resin. The liner and the fibreglass are called the 'pressure vessel', and it is put into an 'outer shroud' – the light grey part, and then there's the green handle. The outside is the decorative part.

What else is important about the pack?
One of the safety features is that it won't explode if there's a fire.

Do you promote the pack's appearance and lightness as key selling points?
Yes, we do, absolutely.

Would you have done anything differently?
We have now produced an internal guidebook for marketing the bottle. Wherever we go we follow a launch process that includes all of the communications, procurement and engagement – everything like that.

Did you encounter any difficulties?
Consumers had difficulty with 'Is it as light, as it is strong, as it is safe?'. And the word 'light' – did this mean that the gas was lighter?

What kind of packs will you produce next?
We're looking at producing different sizes of bottle. The manufacturer is now able to produce a 7.5 kilo [16 ½ pound] bottle. We are looking at doing a 14 kilo [31 pound] one for use on forklift trucks, so extending the product family. And in the future, who knows what other applications – smaller bottles for more mobile use?

02   BP Gas Light in the home. This redesigned gas canister is lightweight, strong, easy to lift and carry and is designed to fit into a domestic environment.

02

Pack　　　**Comme des Garçons
　　　　　 Series 1 perfume**
Client　　**Rei Kawakubo,
　　　　　 Comme des Garçons,
　　　　　 Japan**
Designer **Rei Kawakubo,
　　　　　 Comme des Garçons,
　　　　　 France**
Year　　　**2000**

Series 1: Leaves is the first outcome of Rei Kawakubo's unorthodox explorations into perfume creation. Each series is contained in packs that perform by expressing the essential character of the series and Kawakubo's scientific approach to its creation.

The scents she produces are often described as anti-perfumes and contain synthetic olfactory elements that have been described as cellulose, acetone or mineral carbon. This series of 'green' scents is focused on the aromas of lily and calamus leaves, and the sinister and medicinal smell of smoky black tea.

The range is packaged in industrially styled gas cylinder-shaped containers made of aluminium. These are coated in a shiny, saturated, dense tint of green that is the antithesis of natural. The chrome cap reiterates that the product is modern and unapologetically man-made.

The sans serif type is set in stencil-like capital letters that consolidate the industrial character of the perfumes. The bold, glossy red letters are the colour opposite of the lush green leaves they describe, jarring the eye and setting in motion an uncomfortable visual interference that draws attention back to the pack for another assault on the senses.

03

Pack   **Comme des Garçons
          Series 6 perfume**
Client   **Rei Kawakubo,
          Comme des Garçons,
          Japan**
Designer **Rei Kawakubo,
          Comme des Garçons,
          France**
Year   **2004**

Rei Kawakubo's sixth experiment in fragrance creation has produced a range of five idiosyncratic 'anti-perfumes'. Series 6 is based on the familiar smells of everyday man-made places and things, including dry cleaning, garages, synthetic leather (Skai), soda and tar.

The packs perform by expressing the synthetic theme of the series and by developing the industrial and artificial aesthetics of earlier ones. They celebrate their chemical identity in their translucent polyethylene outer containers and lids, and are elevated from their otherwise commonplace appearance by subtle remodelling that changes their proportions and hones their details to make them slim and reveal the beauty of their internal 'machinery'. Their black plastic innards resemble sinister robotic stomachs that contain, and protect the integrity of, the fragrances.

The utilitarian black, stencilled typography evokes warehouse packaging and maintains the essential industrial character of the series. The filigree of type adds an extra layer of decoration and creates an architectural-like structure, and the illusion of three-dimensional composition that gives the packs their alluring depth.

04

Pack	'The Vanity of Allegory' postcard box set
Client	Guggenheim Museum, Berlin
Designer	Matthias Ernstberger Typography: Marian Bantjes Art Direction: Stefan Sagmeister Production: Lara Fieldbinder and Melissa Secundino, Sagmeister, USA
Year	2005

'The Vanity of Allegory' was a group exhibition organized by the artist Douglas Gordon that explored self-portraiture and artistic vanity. As well as his own works it included contributions by 30 other artists. All of the works were reproduced as postcards and contained in a decorative box.

This strangely shaped printed card container is a portable version of 'The Vanity of Allegory', allowing the postcards to be carried and viewed by visitors as they looked at the artworks. But while the postcards represent the exhibits, the box literally demonstrates the theme of the exhibition: the lid contains an angled mirror that reflects the word 'vanity'.

The black-and-white colour scheme expresses the dialectical relationship of opposites, such as life and death, fact and fiction, that permeated the exhibition. Black also characterizes darkness, death and the urge for immortality through self-representation. The box is divided in two – like a person and his or her image. The typography is an amalgamation of digital pixels derived from hand-drawn Gothic script, expressing ideas about the past and the present, analogue and digital, and real and synthetic. Even the decoration on the box and the luxurious quality of its production could be construed as being self-indulgent and vain.

01　　　　Apple iPod Nano
offers a neutral external packaging,
with the colour coming directly
from the product it contains.

02　　　　Another eyecatching
colour in the iPod Nano range.

02

Case Study
Apple
iPod Nano

Pack　　　　**Apple iPod Nano**
Client　　　**Apple, USA**
Designer　　**Apple, USA**
Year　　　　**2007**

When it comes to pack design Apple is the ultimate performer. The company's total focus on its products means that the primary function of a pack is to connect the consumer with the product as seamlessly as possible and remove any potential barriers between the two.

The transparent and unobtrusive iPod Nano pack reveals the product in a single visual hit that is the first step in the orchestrated process of bringing customer and product together.

Seamlessness is taken to new levels as the iPod appears to hover in space within a perfectly engineered, thickly walled glassy tank, like a mysterious science-fictional device suspended within a futuristic crystalline container. Its name is typeset on the side of the inner card pack, forming an attractive retail display when repeated, and directing the customer to the pack front where the iPod is revealed.

Because the visual appearance of this iconic product is ubiquitous it needs no introduction – the typeset name exists only to educate those not yet initiated into Apple's world.

The pack also performs by echoing the product's materials, rounded curves, clear, chunky plastic bezel and light-reflective contour lines. Extending these design characteristics into the pack diminishes the demarcation between pack and product and lifts the value of the pack closer to that of the iPod. It also allows the customer to preview – and actually feel – the quality of the product before they buy it, without actually touching it. The pack also expands the iPod's small volume to a larger size that can be comfortably handled. In the consumer electronics sector, where small product size is associated with higher value, this presents significant challenges for packaging designers.

Following the orientation of the iPod when it is held the 'right way up' the pack opens intuitively from the top. This prevents the product falling out, and also reveals that it is the radius of the box lid's curves that holds it in position without the need for adhesive or fixings. The lid and main box split in two, emphasizing the thinness of the product compared to the total box depth, and revealing a card container that performs as the iPod's backdrop and a storage space for its stand, earphones, USB cable, two tiny booklets – a 'Quick Start' guide and 'Important Information' – and stickers that are too large for the product and are intended to promote the customer's membership of Apple's 'club'.

This minimal packaging solution may be the result of the need to control costs and waste as Apple's production volumes increase, but it also delivers additional value by providing a physical threshold – a crystal Pandora's box – that dramatizes the customer's entry into Apple's egalitarian design- and innovation-led brand ethos. The pack also protects the iPod from impact damage, and functions ecologically by using sustainable or recyclable materials.

With so few moving components the quality, feel and detail of each part of the pack, and the product, must work perfectly, deliver meaning and be sensorially or emotionally rewarding for the consumer. The extremely high quality of the plastics and paper

01   Apple iPod Nano Quick
Start guide. This tiny booklet is possible
because most of the user information,
typically found in the packaging, is
subsumed within the product.

02   Apple iPod Nano pack,
unpacked. Earphones, USB cable, dock
adapter and guidebook are stored in
a white container that performs as a
backdrop against which the product
is displayed, and also emphasizes the
simplicity that is typical of Apple products.

01

02

engineering and print suggests
that the product's performance
is similarly flawless.
          Despite its fashionable
reputation Apple is a grounded
and disciplined business
with design excellence at the
heart of everything it is and
does. On opening the pack
the first text to be seen is the
statement: 'Designed by Apple
in California.' By describing
the business as being located in
California, rather than in the
United States, the company
has culturally positioned
itself in the progressive
vanguard of the country's
creative industries alongside

film, environmentalism and
liberalism and away from the
conservatism of much of the
rest of America. The words
also cleverly assert Apple's
revolutionary, evolutionary
ethos of placing design before
technology, which is unique in
consumer electronics industries.
          As the company and
its products and technologies
evolve, the relative amount
of packaging it produces will
diminish radically to reduce the
distance between customers and
the Apple-branded experience
– inviting consumers to move
closer, buy more and stay
longer within the company's

ever-expanding online and
retail domains. Multilingual
instruction manuals, statutory
information and warranties
are already subsumed within
many of its products and its
website, and are designed to
be helpful, easy to understand
and user friendly – on its
website they could even be
considered as a new form of
intangible 'packaging' that can
be continually updated and
is available for users to view,
download or print as required.
          Apple has increased
the range of territory
traditionally described as
'packaging', extending it from

03   Apple iPod Nano pack.
With few moving parts, the high
quality of each element of the pack is
designed to express the seamless and
perfect performance of the product.

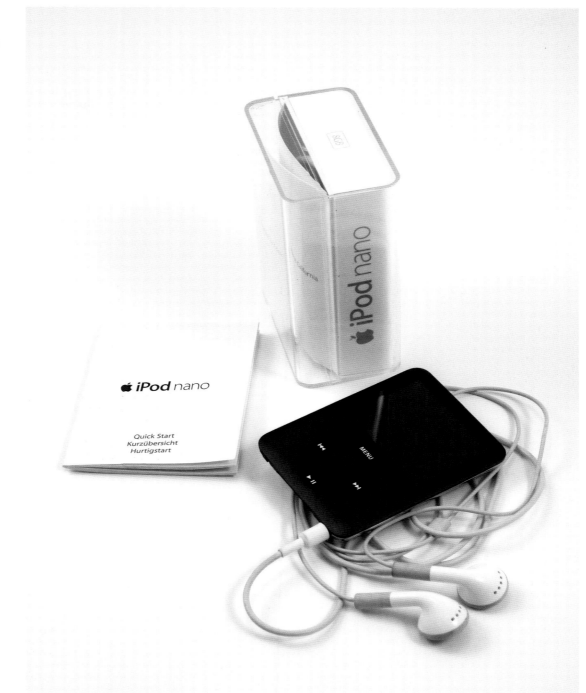

03

the hard-drive deep within the
product, through the interface,
out to the Internet and into
shops, homes and workplaces.
By increasing the scale of the
'unpacking experience', retail
environments such as Apple
Store have given customers
new places where they can
continue the rewarding
process of unpacking the
company's products and
experiencing the expanding
universe of the Apple brand.

06

Pack   **Equerry horse brush**
Client   **Vale Brothers, UK**
Designer   **Vale Brothers, UK**
Year   **2007**

Vale Brothers is the world's largest brush manufacturer and has specialized in horse-grooming products since 1786. This combined product, pack and display performs on many levels. It saves material by incorporating the retail display and information functions within the product; and it makes a virtue of showcasing the brush's high-quality leather construction, prestigious black and red leather, and military styling to express durability, heritage and efficacy. Gold-foil printing further increases the status of the product, which has been given the ultimate endorsement of a royal warrant of appointment, showing that it is the British royal family's horse brush of choice.

This is a natural extension of the brand: 'equerry' is the title of the officer who is charged with caring for the horses of the royal household.

However, the pack is not simply a luxurious decoration. Its leather construction is flexible and makes brushing more comfortable and easy, while the red hand strap contrasts with the black brush to make the product easy to find in a dark, stable environment.

07

Pack   **Guinness® Draught**
Client   **Diageo, Ireland**
Designer **Diageo, UK**
Year   **2006**

Guinness Draught performs its visual trick of looking like a rich, dark chilled drink when it is poured into a glass from an aluminium can. However, this pack is more than just a can; it contains a patented plastic 'widget' device – the Guinness In-Can System – that delivers a perfect pub-quality drink.

When the can is opened the drop in pressure causes the widget to release a jet of beer and nitrogen through a tiny laser-cut hole. This makes the beer surge, settle, look, taste and feel exactly like a fresh drink that has been poured using technology found only in pubs. This packaging innovation, first invented in 1988, revolutionized beer off-sales because it allowed consumers to enjoy a pub-quality drink in the comfort of their own homes.

The graphic design of the can has evolved to reflect changes in the way the beer is consumed. This one celebrates its distinguished history by focusing on its brand, but also acknowledges the fashion for drinking extra-cold beer by adding icy condensation at the base of the pack.

The widget cost over £6.5 million ($9 million) to perfect and more than 800 million cans containing the device have been sold worldwide.

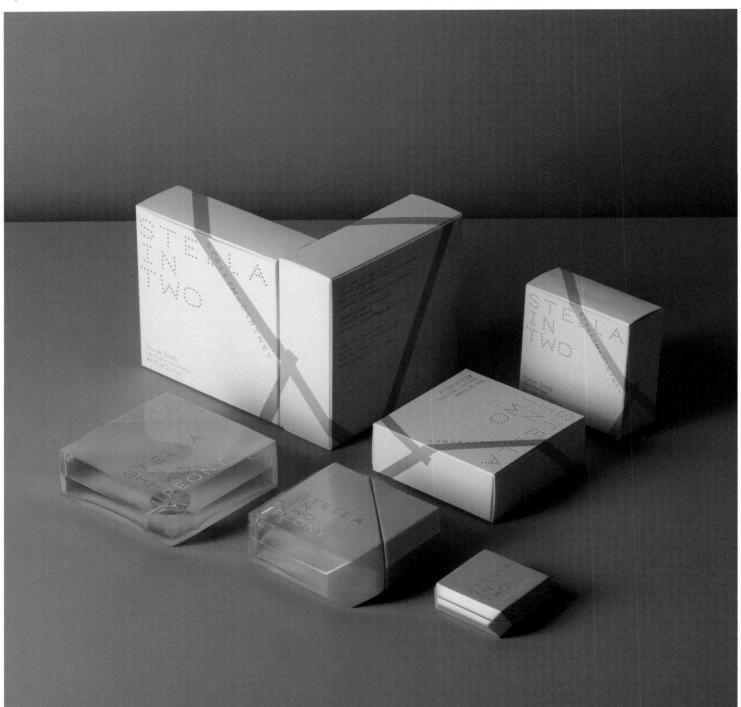

08

Pack　　Stella in Two solid perfume
Client　Stella McCartney, UK
Designer　Paul Austin, Director,
　　　　　MadeThought, UK

Year　　2007

Stella McCartney is a designer's designer, and the graphic branding for this solid perfume compact, which performs in memorable and unconventional ways, features carefully crafted typography composed of dots reminiscent of glamorous theatre lights – but which are also modest and understated like McCartney's intelligent, structured, subtly detailed approach to fashion.

All the Stella McCartney fragrances are in packs that feature softly faceted edges, which are a key element of her brand and are also expressed in the graphic design on her packaging. This talismanic perfume container is made precious by its small size,

the heavy weight of its cast-steel casing and the interplay of asymmetries that expresses the care invested in its creation and its resulting high quality. The debossed typography feels good to touch, and contrasts delicately with the printed type above it.

The pack demands to be handled and explored, and delivers a surprise when it slides horizontally, splitting in half to reveal a shallow pat of solid perfume. When closed with a reassuring and satisfying click, it begs to be touched and turned so that the ever-changing facets of its diamond-cut design can be viewed.

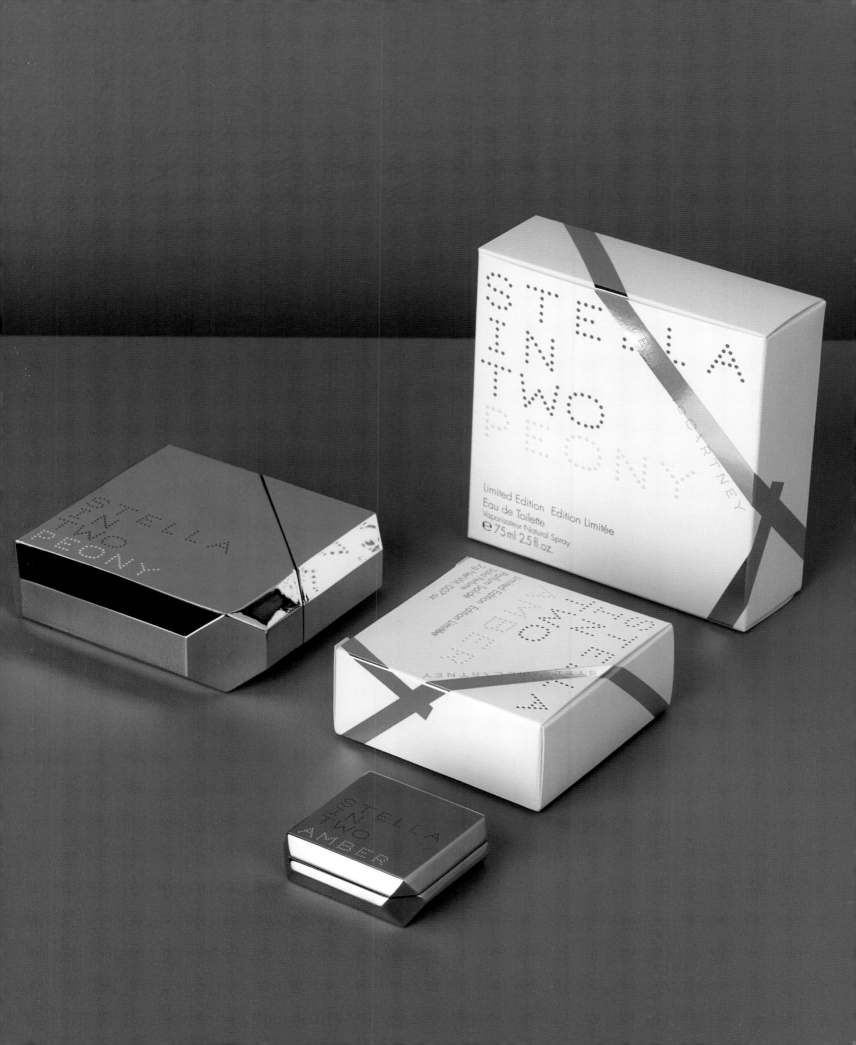

09

Pack	**Liten Ljus Lager**
Client	**Krönleins Bryggeri, Sweden**
Designer	**Amore, Sweden**
Year	**2004**

The pack for Liten Ljus Lager is made from recyclable aluminium and performs by graphically repeating the name of the beer in different typographic ways, and expressing its qualities through colours and materials.

Liten Ljus Lager literally means 'small light lager'. However, the three geometrical 'L'-shaped letters could be interpreted as reiterating 'Lager, Lager, Lager' to ensure there is no mistaking the contents of the can. The diminishing sizes of the decorative 'L'-shapes also dynamically suggest the falling liquid level as if the product was being consumed in three great gulps. Liten Ljus Lager's minimal and ultra-stylish design eschews

tradition and therefore, by inference, also the heritage and craft of brewing, which create flavour. While silver does not express the pale yellow colour of lager it does express 'cold', and low temperatures reduce flavour – so we can assume this is not a beer for connoisseurs; instead it is a great-looking lager designed to be consumed by the fashion-conscious in hot nightclubs.

Few lager packs are black and silver as these colours don't describe the product, but the chic performance of this austere design will not be demeaned or undermined by the drink's more common golden, effervescent image.

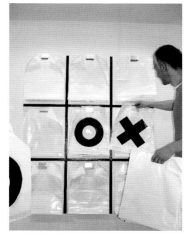

10

Pack   'Signe Quotidiens'
              carrier bags
Client   Centre Culturel Suisse,
              Paris
Designer   Marco Walser and
              Valentin Hindermann,
              Elektrosmog,
              Switzerland
Year   2005

These polythene carrier bags were designed for a Paris-based exhibition to promote Switzerland and its culture, and were also a useful and cost-effective way of enabling people to carry information about the exhibits.

Visitors to the 'Signe Quotidiens' exhibition, held at the Centre Culturel Suisse in Paris, were invited to take a bag decorated with either a nought or a cross from a display that consisted of a grid with nine compartments, like the one used to play the noughts and crosses game. Each compartment contained a rack of the bags, and visitors were encouraged to interact and get to know each other by playing a real game.

The design approach was appropriate because the cross is featured on the Swiss national flag, and linked the design of the bags, and playing noughts and crosses, with Switzerland. The game expressed the country's friendly, playful character and encouraged visitors to see an aspect of its culture that made them feel positive about it. The surreal way in which the bags were used also helped people to feel good about Switzerland long after the exhibition had closed.

01   Ecopod handmade paper
design, showing the dove design
screenprinted onto a blue background.

02   Ecopod coffin in White. The
coffins are designed to biodegrade when
they come into contact with moisture after
they have been buried in the ground.

03   Ecopod coffin in Gold Leaf.
Coffins covered in gold or silver leaf
are sometimes used for night burials,
where their ability to reflect light can
create a powerful theatrical effect.

02

03

Case Study
Ecopod coffin

11

Pack   **Ecopod coffin**
Client   **Ecopod, UK**
Designer **Hazel Selina, UK**
Year   **2007**

Packaging plays a special role in life's great events, including birthdays, marriages and deaths. In death, packaging performs literally, by containing the body in a traditionally designed outer box that becomes the focus of a ceremony that dramatizes and marks the life and death of a person. Historically, the process of wrapping a corpse in a shroud and placing it within a robust or decorative box was part of the theatre of burial – of the ceremonial honouring, celebrating, and grieving for, the dead.

By comparison, Ecopod is a modern container that fulfils its traditional role as a robust and reverential package for a person, and also offers additional environemental performance. It takes its design inspiration from the shapes of ancient Egyptian sarcophagi and on organic forms found in the natural word. It is made from papier mâché – a mixture of paper pulp and glue that can be formed into almost any shape.

The papier mâché outer box and the fabric lining are made from 100 per cent eco-friendly naturally derived materials. All paints and glues come from ethical companies and are free from chemicals. The coffin is designed to biodegrade when it is exposed to moisture after it is buried in the ground, and it meets the European Union's rigorous emissions requirements for crematoria, ensuring that it performs environmentally as well as culturally. The coffin has also passed tests to make sure it is strong enough to carry the weight of a person without breaking or cracking.

While the market for environmentally friendly cardboard coffins is growing, many manufacturers simply produce printed cardboard copies of traditional coffins that look cheap and inferior by comparison with Ecopod.

Interview with Hazel Selina, Designer, Ecopod

When did you first begin to design the Ecopod?
Sixteen years ago.

Has the shape evolved?
I think I've now found the perfect shape. I didn't want it to hark back to the past but I also had a very deep interest in organic form and ancient Egypt. I did a lot of drawing and I made a lot of clay maquette shapes before I ended up with the shape I've got.

Do you design any other products?
The only other thing I do is an acorn urn. Again, when people get cremated the ashes go into a horrible large plastic container that looks like a coffee pot made out of red or brown plastic. It's very polluting and takes a thousand years to biodegrade. I designed an acorn made out of papier mâché that biodegrades really easily.

It's a really optimistic shape.
I see death as a rebirth into another reality. I just wanted to help people because it's such a somber, awful event – often in a crematorium and over in 20 minutes.

01   Ecopod coffin in Indigo Blue.
In addition to meeting stringent legal
standards, these containers also perform
as the centrepiece of the burial ritual.

02   Ecopod coffin in Forest Green.
Ecopod coffins perform environmentally
by being made of 100% recycled paper.
They are 100% recyclable and produce
no toxins when incinerated or buried.

03   Ecopod coffin in Indian Red.
The coffins can be individually decorated
to reflect the character of the deceased or
silkscreen printed with designs depicting
doves, an Aztec sun or a Celtic cross.

01

02

03

It's like an anachronistic Victorian tradition that's simply persisted.
Yes, that's right. I wanted to help people create a celebration of the life that was lived, and I thought if I made something colourful it might help make the funeral a bit more uplifting – at least, that was my aim.

Why did you design the gold-leaf version?
We thought we'd do one with a bit of 'bling' to it. It is covered in gold leaf. We do a silver-leaf version as well – it takes the boys two days to overlay it with the leaf. It's quite a big job. I always

thought it would be fantastic for night funerals with people carrying burning torches.

That's very dramatic! Do you design bespoke versions?
Yes, we do personalize coffins. Because of the material – you can pin it, staple it, whatever – sometimes we put sculptural things on them. I sent one out the other day with a huge pair of white paper sculptured wings on it.

How long does it take to make a coffin?
Three a week at the most.

How many people participate in the manufacturing process?
Just two young men in the workshop. People like the coffins so much sometimes we have to turn them away because we can't fulfil the orders. We're now looking for a factory that can machine-make them so that we can sell them more cheaply and produce more. But it's a real job to find a factory that's got the machinery because, apart from using it for pallets, no one in the world is working with papier mâché at this size.

04   Ecopod handmade paper
design, with Celtic cross design
screenprinted onto a green background.

05   Ecopod handmade paper
design, showing the Aztec sun design
screenprinted onto a red background.

06   Arka Acorn Urn. This urn,
made of handmade paper, expresses the
idea of woodland burial and is designed
to contain the ashes after cremation.

06

04

05

*How did you develop the
stability of the material?*
I did all the tests in my
kitchen, using my oven and
liquidizers and testing different
hardeners to get the mix right.

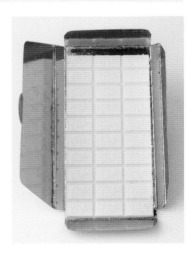

12

Pack   **Chocolats Rohr**
Client   **Chocolats Rohr,
Switzerland**
Designer   **Chocolats Rohr,
Switzerland**
Year   **2007**

These sumptuously coloured card wrappers are embellished with Rohr's logotype in gold metallic foil, which gives each of the 22 packs their hallmark of quality. The mixture of typefaces reveals how they have evolved, and reassures the consumer that the products are authentic.

Each flavour is distinguished by a different hue, and when these are displayed together they create a colourful rainbow in the store. The uneven appearance of the colours is because a standard four-colour process rather than a bespoke single colour of ink is used for printing – an indicator of a genuinely vernacular product. The packs are then gloss laminated to evoke the luscious lacquered appearance of chocolate.

The highlight of a pack's performance is when it is opened in a single movement to reveal the chocolate lying on a tray of pure gold that appears to glow from within. Each square is embossed with the Rohr logotype, extending the packaging into the product. The other surprise is that the pack is made from one sheet of stiff card. Moving from pack to chocolate in a single bold step signals that this product is for experts who do not need an elaborate unwrapping experience to convince them that Rohr make the best chocolates in Geneva.

13

Pack	Vitra Eames Plywood Elephant Anniversary limited edition
Client	Vitra, Germany
Designer	Elephant: Charles and Ray Eames, USA Box: Vitra, Germany
Year	Elephant: 1945 Box: 1945

This limited edition of a twentieth-century design icon performs by extending the audience for the product by producing collectable miniatures that are attractive and valuable keepsakes.

In the 1940s the designer Charles Eames and his wife Ray invented a method of moulding plywood to create furniture and sculptures. Their Plywood Elephant sculpture achieved legendary status among collectors as it was never commercially produced. Only two prototypes were made and displayed at New York's Museum of Modern Art; now only one exists, owned by the Eames family.

Founded in France in 1950, Vitra manufactures high-quality furniture created by some of the world's most famous designers. To commemorate the 100th anniversary of the birth of Charles Eames, it manufactured 2,000 collector's editions of the Plywood Elephant, each numbered and packed in a little wooden crate with a sliding lid.

The crate is made from the same birch wood as the elephant, thereby extending the characteristics of the product into the pack and elevating its value, which is further endorsed by an edition number that makes it, too, collectable. The unfinished quality of the wood used for the crate reminds collectors of the raw material used by Charles and Ray in the innovative lamination process that was used to create the elephant.

The black screen-printed condensed san serif type is a gently humorous reference to a tea chest or cargo case, and too beautiful to hide in a cupboard. The pack's sliding lid recalls old-fashioned pencil boxes, and evokes the period in which the Eames worked and the tools they used. Inside, the little elephant is nestled in shredded paper, like a real animal in a tiny straw bed. A folded paper information sheet, designed to echo the Modernist graphics of the 1950s, explains the context for the project.

14

Pack | **Deutsche See Fisch-Box**
Client | **Deutsche See, Germany**
Designer | **Feldmann + Schultchen Design Studios, Germany**
Year | **2007**

Industrial fish boxes are normally lifeless, utilitarian containers that smell of dead fish and do not enhance the sparkling silver catch they contain. Nor do they communicate information such as the condition of the product or assist in its processing, distribution or retail display.

The Deutsche See box simultaneously performs in all these ways. Instead of being a dull, angular freight container it uses high-density polyethylene (HDPE) to create the impression of freshness by evoking the ocean – its translucent blueness and the rippling waves on its surface – like a slice of the sea. The box is designed to stack securely and easily when full and to nest in the minimum of space when empty. Its internal volume ensures that the contents are efficiently packed and are displayed in a curved pattern like a live shoal of fish, which also suggests freshness.

Its many patented features include clear labelling, and a temperature-monitoring system that helps with the accurate control of storage and freezing. Perforations allow meltwater to cascade away, preserving the fish and removing bad smells. The reduction in overall box volume compared to that of traditional containers, and the pack's compatibility with manufacturing equipment, are among the many innovations that have ensured the success of the Deutsche See box.

15

Pack   *Helvetica* film pack
Blu-ray limited edition
'record' package
Client   Plexifilm, USA
Designer   Experimental Jetset,
the Netherlands
Year   2008

Every aspect of this graphic masterpiece is focused on extending the audience for this 'product' – a documentary film about Max Miedinger's Helvetica typeface, directed by Gary Hustwit – through 1,500 copies of this limited edition package.

The pack includes a 12 inch gatefold record cover that contains a four-panel Blu-ray disc insert in one side and a fold-out poster on the other. All are presented in a bespoke black cloth 'record' bag. The design evokes an old-fashioned typographic specimen sheet and features the alphabet typeset in Helvetica – one of the world's most ubiquitous typefaces. This is chopped up, forcing the user to scrutinize its characteristic shapes, which are further contrasted and their details emphasized by being rendered in black and white.

The pack is based on the idea of different formats – suggested by Gary Hustwit, who described the film as a 'rock documentary about a typeface'. The limited edition contains a high-definition digital film in Blu-ray disc format, about 'the' typeface, Helvetica, packaged in a card sleeve and outer bag in the same vinyl record format. The resulting package makes the user question whether to store it in a record collection, put it in a bookcase or hang it on a wall.

**LEVI'S
PREMIUM COLLECTION
ACCESSORIES**

16

Pack   **Levi's® knock-down
packs**
Client   **Drexel University, USA**
Designer   **Kyle Cook, USA**
Year   **2007**

The idea behind this ingenious packaging system was to create a series of simple, innovative and functional packs that would support the classic Levi's brand and enhance the retail experience.

The packs fold flat so that they can be stored in the space below the retail counter, and are sized to accommodate Levi's range of clothing, including a carrying box for jeans, a gift box for smaller items such as watches, belts, hats and wallets, and a 'standard' bag for shirts, jackets, T-shirts and jumpers. The jeans bag is made from stiff printed card with deep gusset folds on either side that increase its structural strength. Slots are die-cut into both sides, allowing a wooden dowel that spans the width of the bag to be inserted. Jeans are folded in half and hung over the dowel so that they don't become creased on their journey from store to home. The result is a unique packaging experience that engages staff and customers in a branded performance.

The packs feature Levi's logotypes but also use a dark brown denim pattern, and a contrasting jewel-coloured illustration showing a customer wearing jeans, thereby completing the retail performance and promoting the company's core product.

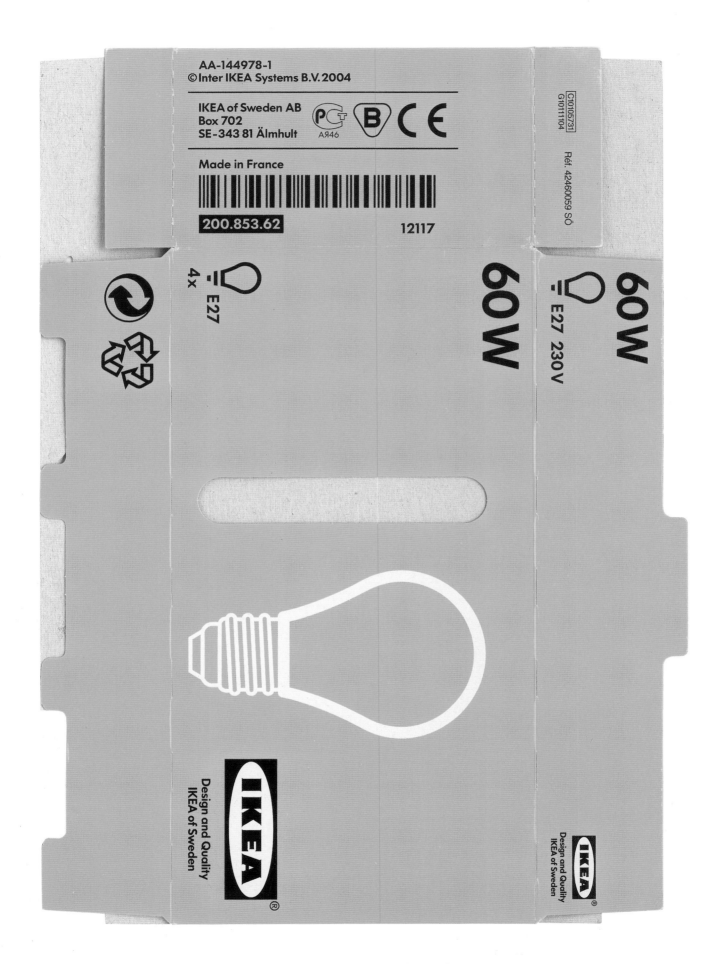

AA-144978-1
© Inter IKEA Systems B.V. 2004

IKEA of Sweden AB
Box 702
SE-343 81 Älmhult

Made in France

200.853.62   12117

60W

60W

E27 230V

E27
4x

Design and Quality
IKEA of Sweden

Design and Quality
IKEA of Sweden

Réf. 42460059 SÖ

01   IKEA GLODA 4x60W screw-in
light bulbs. These packs communicate
effectively and efficiently by using symbols.

02   IKEA GLODA 60W and
40W screw-in light bulbs with reflectors.
These radiantly bright containers
look like switched-on light bulbs and
explain their contents by forming
an electrifying repeat pattern.

03   IKEA SPARSAM
compact energy-saving twin tube.
These packs express their 'green'
credentials using their green colour.

Case Study
IKEA household goods

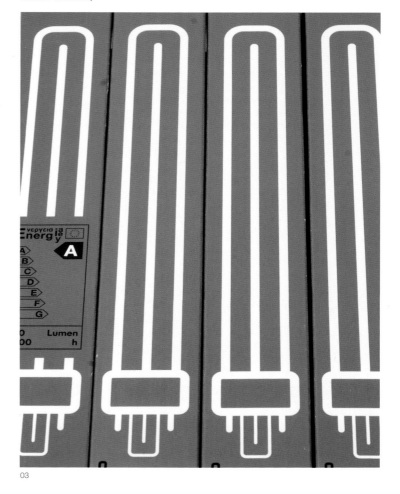

03

02

17

Pack	IKEA household goods
Client	IKEA, Sweden
Designer	IKEA, Sweden
Year	2007

IKEA's frugal ethos produces iconic packaging that is clever, attractive and practical, and performs economically and environmentally.
GLODA light bulbs have a golden yellow glow and the SPARSAM energy-saving bulbs are green in colour and also in their contribution to the environment. Both packs describe their contents graphically and metaphorically, using colour and decorative line drawings that form a large, eye-catching repeat pattern when they are displayed on the retail shelf.
ALKALISK batteries match their yellow packaging perfectly, making it hard to determine where the product ends and the pack begins. They also capitalize on their luminous shelf presence to attract customers and sales.
The packaging for SMAL drinks stirrers and DRAGON teaspoons demonstrate that simple is effective. These everyday commodities are presented in straightforward black-and-white card packs that focus attention on the products and on the high-quality typesetting and composition that comprise their design.

The monochrome beauty of SYNTES KONST ceramic bowls is not obscured by the cleverly designed bands that simultaneously communicate product information, permit bowls to be displayed together as a set and protect them from damage when they are transported. This cost-effective single-colour printed card solution is also completely recyclable.
IKEA packaging performs in many different ways. The company was the first retailer in the UK to stop using polythene carrier bags and offer reusable alternatives such as their large ISIG bags. All the packs carry stylish symbols that eloquently describe different aspects of the products, their care and use, to customers in 36 countries.
The company also names the designers of the products on the packs. It's good to know there's a person, or a team, behind our teaspoons, sofas and tables, and it's also good to know who to blame if they don't perform!

Interview with Charlie Brown, Environmental Manager, IKEA UK

How does IKEA approach its packaging design?
From 'resource efficiency'. The less packaging we use, the less it contributes to our costs. Frugality is part of our DNA. Ingvar Kamprad's *Testament to a Retailer*, written in the 1970s, which is a mission statement for our organization, talks about profit bringing us resources and low-cost profiling. He says that 'the waste of resources is one of the greatest diseases of mankind'. We come from an area in southern Sweden called Småland where the people are renowned for being frugal and making the best of every resource.
In the 1950s or early 1960s when we first started to flat-pack furniture it wasn't about environmentalism. It was about economies of scale, and the flat-pack concept came from there. It's environmentally positive – the more things you get on a truck the fewer trucks and raw materials you use. We have packaging technicians in Sweden. They spend all of their time working out how you can get the most parts into a box

01   IKEA symbols transcend verbal
language and perform by communicating
effectively with customers in 36 countries.

02   IKEA DRAGON packs of
6 coffee spoons.

03   ALKALINE packs of
10 batteries.

02

01

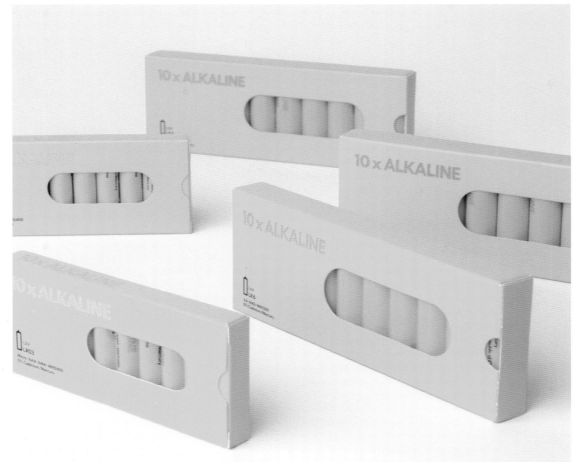

03

with the minimum amount of packaging around them.

Which adds value to the customer's perception of the product?
If you've ever opened one of our boxes which has maybe got a fairly complicated piece of furniture inside it, and you see how it's been packed and designed, you wouldn't be able to put it back together, ever. It's like a Rubik's cube in reverse. We did a packaging competition a few years ago where we asked the co-workers (IKEA employees) to come up with some ideas for packaging 'tea lights'.

They used to be loosely dumped into a bag. Now they're packed in 100s, shrink-wrapped into a square block with five in a column. That saves us 30 per cent space in transportation.

We also brought in a 'loading ledge' – a preformed plastic 'L-shaped item about half a metre [20 inches] long and 10 centimetres [4 inches] on each edge. These slot on to the sides of boxes and are banded around the outside, so the box becomes the rigid structure, which means we don't have to use palettes. When you cut the banding

strap the plastic ledges drop off and the boxes go on the shelf. Someone then said, 'Hold on a minute, we're using these ledges and a banding strap and we're having to buy locking devices to lock the banding straps.' So they designed a locking device integrated into the loading ledge – a whole transport solution in one item. And when we've finished with them the damaged ones are sent back to the distribution centres and they're shredded and turned into a product that we sell in the store.

04   IKEA SYNTES KONST
2x bowls. These packs perform by
using minimal material – a simple
interlocking paper band – to protect
the product from damage while also
communicating its key features.

04

*I like your packaging symbols
because they're really clear.*
They're really clear because
we have to get an image
to translate in 36 different
countries. Our solutions have
to translate, as a supplier in
Slovakia might be sending
the same packaging to
Germany, Holland and North
America. This probably
has its own brand value.

18

Pack   **Wonderwall Brick Tissue
             Box by Nepia**
Client   **Oji Nepia Company,
             Japan**
Designer   **Art direction: Masamichi
             Katayama, Wonderwall
             Graphic design:
             Groovisions
             Creative Agency: Dentsu,
             Japan**
Year   **2006**

Oji Nepia manufactures disposable paper products, including ranges of specially designed limited edition luxury tissues.

Historically, paper has played a central role in Japanese culture and has been used as a building material, in furniture and lighting production and as a highly valued material in art and calligraphy. Today, the country is the world's third largest consumer of paper after the United States and China, with each person using around 250 kilograms (551 pounds) each year. Land values in Japan are high and there is little flat land on which to build. Consequently, homes are small and every item

placed within their valuable interior space must perform. These printed-card tissue boxes express Japan's cultural links with paper and perform a visual joke: they exploit their generic building-brick proportions by disguising themselves as terracotta bricks.

Wonderwall has conceptualized and art directed this original packaging project, which also reflects the name of the company. Groovisions designed five different versions of the box, using ten variations of brick illustrations that could be stacked together to create the illusion of a brick wall. In doing so they transformed an otherwise mundane product, which is usually covered or stored in a cupboard, into a desirable

and collectable accessory for the home that functions simultaneously as an ironic artwork.

19

Pack   Molton Brown
            Thai Vert Aircandela
Client   Molton Brown, UK
Designer   Molton Brown, UK
Year   2005

The room fragrance candle in a valuable hand-blown glass holder, and the gift box that contains them, perform as a prestigious, immaculately crafted luxury present.

The card and paper box is skilfully made using traditional techniques and materials derived from bookbinding. Embossed paper is drawn tightly over, and glued to, a sturdy card carcass and the edges are neatly turned over and hidden behind a paper lining. The paper is screen-printed, with the logotype rendered in a contrasting glossy ink finish that shines when it catches the light and animates the package's retail 'performance'. The recessed pack front mirrors the turned-edge construction of the box to create a substantial lid that can be extracted by pulling a loop of screen-printed grosgrain ribbon. The use of grosgrain, which is normally used in the structure and decoration of evening or ceremonial garments, emphasizes the product's impeccable construction and prestige.

Inside the box the candle and holder are secured in a tight-fitting die-cut card frame that prevents both from being damaged and displays them centre-stage.

Because the candle lasts for up to 80 hours the box performs as a safe container throughout its lifetime, and can then be used to store the candle-holder.

20

Pack   Schönberg
            Ensemble Edition
Client   Schönberg Ensemble,
            the Netherlands
Designer   André Cremer,
            UNA designers,
            the Netherlands
Year   2007

The Schönberg Ensemble is famous for performing the works of many of the twentieth century's best-known avant-garde composers, including those of Arnold Schönberg, Karlheinz Stockhausen and Michel van der Aa.

The Schönberg Ensemble Edition is a mammoth retrospective that covers a century of musical composition and features the ensemble's total repertoire, packaged in a single boxed edition that comprises 22 CDs, three DVDs and a 628-page bilingual book. The design of the whole pack expresses the experimental nature of the music it contains to create an exciting three-dimensional graphic feast that is a dynamic performance in itself. The slipcase and book cover feature rough-textured grey board that contrasts with the smooth-textured CD covers, which are arranged to create a graduated rainbow of colours that could be said to describe the huge variety of music the edition represents.

The striated pattern of horizontal lines used on the CD and DVD covers translates the atonality of Modernist music into contemporary digital design. When the covers are viewed together they present a variable but harmonious single entity.

Each of the book's 22 chapter openers features one of the CD cover designs in monochrome, with the lines bleeding to the fore-edge of the page where they act as a visually playful thumb index.

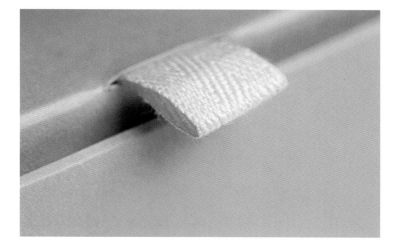

21

Pack   **Woolrich clothing packs**
Client   **Woolrich, USA**
Designer   **D-sign, Italy**
Year   **2008**

Woolrich was founded by John Rich in 1830, in Pennsylvania, and is renowned for its rugged outdoor clothing and iconic red-and-black plaid Buffalo Shirts – named, by Rich, in honour of his buffalo herd.

These special packs are for customers and the press, and contain gifts such as scarves or bags, and invitations to Woolrich events, including fashion shows and art exhibitions. They perform by exploiting techniques and materials that express the company's distinguished history as the United States' oldest wool mill, and celebrate its famous fabrics.

The packs create an appropriate context for Woolrich's historic logo and its frontier-style slab serif typeface by featuring matt-finished unbleached card, natural cotton rope, linen tape and metal studs – materials that look old and emphasize the company's nineteenth-century origins. They are also carefully chosen to evoke the fabrics used in the new season's designer collection.

Untying and unwrapping a Woolrich box signals that it contains a precious gift. This is underlined by the use of sensual materials and the high quality of paper engineering and print – mirrored by the company's products – which make the packs too good to throw away. As well as acknowledging the past, they are effective presents in themselves, and sustainable, reusable and recyclable keepsakes.

22

Pack   **Ramune bottles**
Client   **Sangaria Beverage**
          Company, Japan
Designer **Ramune, Japan**
Year   **2007**

This intriguing glass and plastic pack for a popular carbonated drink performs like a transparent mechanical machine. It visually reveals the pressures exerted by the carbon dioxide used to create effervescence, and so expresses the power of Ramune's thirst-quenching fizziness.

This modern redesign of the old-fashioned Codd-neck bottles uses a glass marble enclosure to contain the gas. Invented by Hiram Codd in 1872, the bottles were largely replaced by ones with crimped metal tops, and aluminium cans. Ramune is unique in retaining and modernizing the design to make it appeal to a new generation of consumers by applying transparent, shrink-wrapped printed plastic sleeves that are easily and frequently changed.

In order to open the bottle the marble is pushed inwards to release the gas, using a plastic device. The squashed neck has two 'pockets' that hold the marble and stop it rattling around while the drink is consumed. However, trapping the marble in the pockets requires practice, and lots of noisy marble-rattling – a familiar sound throughout Japan's long hot summers – in order to enjoy a silent, smooth drink.

Promote

Overview
Packaging that Promotes

The global growth of brands and the design industries that
create them has produced a legion of managers responsible
for maintaining the appearance of the familiar products
and services we see, touch, hear, recognize, trust and buy.
Over the late nineteenth and early twentieth centuries this
branded communication has escalated in its application,
complexity and reach to encompass almost every corner of
civilization in its quest to sell more. In doing so it has shaped
environments, culture, language and behaviour. It has also
driven the evolution of packaging as a conduit for brands and
the promotion of products and services, and the real and virtual
retail environments in which they are displayed and sold.

It didn't take long for brands to become much
more than burnt marks on animal hide. In the past 150 years
they've transcended mere graphic marks that differentiated
one manufacturer from another; brands today are complex
multidimensional amalgamations of visual, aural, haptic,
olfactory, verbal and temporal communication – and written
language – that eloquently transmit their meaning in the blink
of an eye. What's more amazing is that these 'packages' of
information have become a whole new shorthand language
that we eloquently, and often unconsciously, 'speak'. But
what's this got to do with boxes and bags? Let me explain.

Brands are a confection of everything a company, product
or service is and does, including its logotype, tone of voice, values,
how it answers the telephone, how it treats its employees, and
so on. Designers create branded systems of communication
to ensure all aspects of a company's business, and thereby its
brand, are consistently and systematically expressed so that its
outputs are recognized. If these systems are used often enough,
and well enough, the company, or its products or services,
become a brand. Brands are rarely born overnight; they are
usually built according to carefully planned programmes. Their
success depends on being recognized and desired by consumers,
and this 'education' takes time and money or ingenuity.

Packaging gives brands three-dimensi
animation and the ability to communicate simul
many elements of their design. You know it's C
the red colour, white type, bottle shape, logotyp
language. But when Coke is poured from its ico
into a paper cup it loses its form, its identity and
recognized this and promoted its 'taste challen
consumers to distinguish the flavour of its prod
its competitors' drinks, and thereby extended it
new oral dimension. Brands, products and pac
so inextricably linked that it's hard to tell where
ends and the product begins. Over the years A
the boundaries between hardware, software, o
consumer electronics and online services – diss
demarcations between products and packs, an
its brand in every molecule of its output. Protec
have diminished in size and environmental impa
instruction manuals, statutory information and v
been subsumed within product hard drives – m
by intuitive interfaces that bring consumers clos
company and the branded experience of living

Put simply, Apple has extended the te
described as 'packaging'. This brilliant and lucr
land-grab has deepened customers' experienc
relationship with, Apple – and the company has
extending its reach via the Internet and high str
going deep within a product, packaging has ev
beyond it. By increasing the scale of the 'out-of
experience, new environments, like Apple Store
where customers can further 'unpack' and exp

Promotional packaging is about much
neatly crafted, attractive containers. It is a Troja
integrates graphic and three-dimensional desig
that makes it straightforward for businesses to
boundaries of their brands, increasing their valu
and lifespan. It's no accident that designers des
external shape of a pack as the 'envelope' – an
container with the potential to encapsulate an i
number of messages that persuade customers

01   Apple MacBook Pro, by Apple, USA, 2006. Apple products meld seamlessly with their packaging to promote the Apple brand.

02   Andres Sarda Lingerie, by Mucho, Spain, 2007. This gold foiled card pack mirrors its sparkling contents and promotes the luxurious quality of these sexy sequinned knickers.

03   Korres Lip Butters, by K2design and Helene Prablanc, Korres, Greece, 2007. The saturated colour of the photographic outer pack promotes the product's sensual natural ingredients while carefully crafted typographic composition reinforces its premium value.

04   Selfridges own brand food packaging, by R Design, UK, 2007. These chic packs use their sophisticated black colouring and simple bright, modern typography to express their fashionable credentials and premium value.

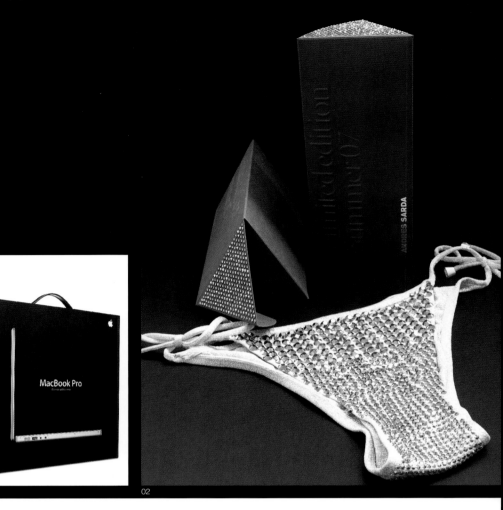

01

02

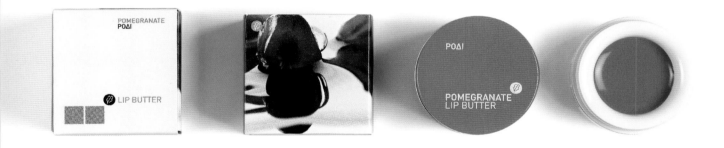

03

04

05   Nikka Whisky, by
Michael Young, China, 2008.
The unique rugged profile of this
bottle prototype helps to distinguish
and promote this brand of whisky.

06   Saks Fifth Avenue
own brand packaging, by Michael
Bierut, Pentagram, USA, 2007.
Sak's eye-catching black-and-white
palette ensures their brand remains
visible even when it contains other
famous luxury branded packs.

07   Xocoa Bonbonera gourmet
chocolates. The richly contrasting minimal
design of this integrated product and pack
helps to focus attention on the flavour
and texture of this premium product.

08   Espa, by Domenic
Lippa, Pentagram, UK, 2006.
Espa's tactile packs and contrasting
relaxing-energizing colour palette
promotes the sensual and temporal
experience of visiting a spa.

09   Sake bottle for Fukunishiki
Company, by Graph, Japan, 2005.
Issay Kitagawa adds value by
presenting this traditional product
in a minimal modern pack.

10   Vine Parma, by Raya
Ivanovskaya, Russia, 2008.
This unusual ethnic-inspired label is
designed to distinguish a small range
of wines from market competitors.

08

05

06

07

10

09

01   The Food Doctor glass, plastic and paper packs. The colour palette promotes these products' natural credentials using green and their healthy benefits by using 'medical' white.

02   The Food Doctor Essential Oil products in 250ml (8.5 ounce) glass bottles. Simple modern label composition and san serif typography give these packs a pharmaceutical demeanour.

Case Study
The Food Doctor health range

02

Pack	The Food Doctor health range
Client	The Food Doctor, UK
Designer	R Design, UK
Year	2006

The Food Doctor products encourage customers to change the way they eat in order to improve their lives, and the packaging is heavily branded to promote this new generation of healthy foods. The company's 'nutrionist's pantry' ideology is promoted verbally and visually by using brand name, typography, colour and composition.

The printed card packs with clear plastic windows feature The Food Doctor brand name typeset in undecorated sans serif capital letters. These express the product's authoritative demeanour, like a doctor prescribing a medicine. The strongest and largest word is FOOD, written in black and reiterating that the product is firstly a food and secondly about health. DOCTOR is proportionately smaller and its meaning is literally and ideologically changed by its green colour.

The medical aspect of the brand is further underpinned by the packs' crisp white background and structured composition with information compartmentalized, in the same manner as on pharmaceutical packs, in order to communicate clearly and systematically. This structured approach uses an undecorated, factual presentation style to deliver both promotional and factual information, mixing the two and thereby powerfully persuading customers of the product's efficacy. The packs also cleverly move nutritional information to a prominent position on the pack front, where it is mixed with promotional claims, such as high fibre or protein source, but does not provide detailed facts and figures, compelling customers to trust the 'doctor's' authority.

Substantial use of green ink promotes the brand's wholesome and natural characteristics. It also contrasts with the medical elements of The Food Doctor to help locate the packs within the food genre. This is further emphasized by the transparent panels, which reveal glimpses of tasty-looking foods that add an appetizing texture. Bright strips of colour are used to differentiate each product, moderate the medical message and confirm that the packs contain foods that are fun to eat.

Interview with Dave Richmond,
Creative Director, R Design

How did the project begin?
Food Doctor came to us about five or six years ago and all they had was a book that they had written. The two authors were both nutritionists and they wanted to create a brand. So, from that, we developed everything for them. At that time nobody was using green, so we chose green because we thought it was natural. And, strangely enough, no one had really captured that and now everyone's fallen in love with it.

We designed their identity and their branding, and their packaging and advertising, their tone of voice and their back-of-pack information. When we presented the first concepts they said, 'It looks like a detergent – nobody uses green'. And we had to convince them that green was their colour because it was natural, it's organic.

01　　　　The Food Doctor 500g
(17.6 ounce) Perfect start cereal packs.
Clear plastic panels reveal and promote
the product's wholesome fibre content.

02　　　　260g (9.1 ounce) tubs and
150g (5.2 ounces) shaker. A consistent
approach to layout, type and colour helps
to promote The Food Doctor brand.

02

01

Why do you use white?
It was an obvious thing to do.
It's medical, but it's not
medical. It's a great name –
The Food Doctor. 'Doctor'
is always about medicine
so we changed the word to
green and 'food' to black.

*I like the large-scale nutritional
information on the front of the pack.*
Our clients are experts in
their field, which is nutrition.
And their brand needed to be
authoritative. I thought this was
really important, so we gave
this aspect some real strength
of character. Some brands don't

do that. Instead they work
on creating a big personality
and some entertainment,
but this is about real food.

*Is there anything you would
change about this project if
you could do it again?*
The Food Doctor is a proper
brand and it will change. It
will change as time goes on,
so I could never be happy
with it because the market's
changing too. At the moment
it's fine, but in two years it
might look different. It will
still have the same logotype
and it will still feel the same

but it will have changed. It's
changed a few times already
over the past five or six years.
Inevitably, the market will
catch up and we'll need to
change again. All brands
have to change according to
how the market changes.

Is colour a big feature of your work?
Yes. We aim for clarity and
simplicity, and we also think
about what to take off the
pack rather than what else
to add to it. It's always about
the minimum amount of
things we can put on a pack
to actually communicate with

03 The Food Doctor 45g (1.5 ounce) bars. These packs use illustrations to quickly communicate and promote the product's natural ingredients.

04 300g (10.5 ounce) Seed mix tubs. In addition to the primary colours of the brand a supplementary colour palette is used to differentiate similar-looking products and packs.

04

03

the consumer. The strongest messages are the simplest.

Packaging is a dying art. It's not the sexiest thing to design right now, and I don't know why. There are not a lot of good packaging designers left. It's important that designers consider what they do and why they're doing it, and try to communicate using the pack because we only have three or four seconds to do this when people scan the retail shelves.

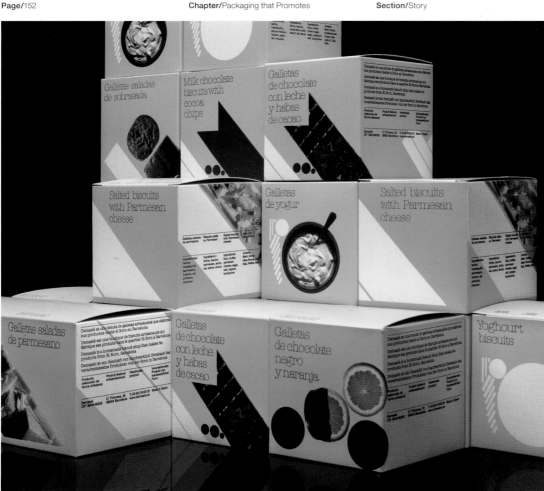

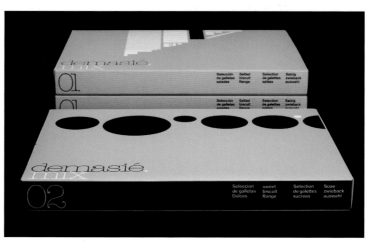

02

Pack   **Demasié biscuits**
Client   **Demasié, Spain**
Designer   **Mucho, Spain**
Year   **2008**

After establishing their landmark chocolate venture, Xocoa (see page 177), Marc and Miguel Escursell worked with their designers, Mucho, to create Demasié, Barcelona's sumptuous and sophisticated biscuit shop.

Mucho's packaging design features an enigmatic circular mark that could describe a Florentine biscuit or an abstract landscape. In fact, it represents an imaginary map of all the different types of biscuit that will ever exist. The mark forms the retail backdrop, and sections of it are featured on each pack to create a distinctive visual identity that promotes the physical elements of Demasié, linking them to create a homogenous entity.

A simple, fresh and chocolate-coloured palette works with the curvaceous lines of American Typewriter Light font, supported by Akzidenz Grotesk, to contrast and complement the bold circles and squares that characterize the round biscuits and bars of chocolate.

Demasié's brand is based on its core product: luxury biscuits. Because biscuits are not popular in Spain, where they are associated with low-quality products found in supermarkets, Mucho had to persuade customers to see them from a new perspective. Packaging was vital in achieving this because it tangibly added value to the product and convinced people that Demasié biscuits are premium quality and deliciously different.

Pack   **Espa spa products**
Client   **Espa, UK**
Designer   **Domenic Lippa,**
              Pentagram Design, UK
Year   **2006**

Espa worked closely with Pentagram to design a branded approach to their packaging that would visually connect their spa interiors and treatments with their products, and ensure that the packs reflect a client's experience when visiting one of their establishments.

The elegant result of the 12-month design process is simple and classic, but has a contemporary twist that characterizes Espa's focus on innovation and its emphasis on discovery – expressed in the journey of travelling through, and opening, the boxes.

The luxurious, relaxing, rich dark colour palette with zingy pink highlights performs the essential role of linking the packs with the claret-coloured spa interiors. The colours proved to be technically challenging and required careful matching across a range of materials, including printed card and paper, plastics and interior finishes. The graduated pink striped pattern suggests the temporal and rhythmic experience of a spa treatment that varies in intensity to gradually relax or invigorate the body and mind. The sensuous tactile qualities of the materials, and the ceremony of unwrapping and using the products, mirrors aspects of Espa's philosophy and spa ritual.

By systematically extending all aspects of their brand throughout the business Espa can promote its brand more consistently and effectively.

04

Pack   **The Fine Cheese Co.
         fruit purées**
Client   **The Fine Cheese Co., UK**
Designer **Julian Roberts,
         Irving Designs, UK**
Year   **2005**

These little jars are special because their visual branding and packaging are designed to modernize their contents – purées of old-fashioned fruits – and promote them as distinctive products in a contemporary deli market.

The chunky little goat's cheese-sized glass jars with metal screw-top lids relate these packs to The Fine Cheese Co.'s other condiments, such as jams and chutneys, but their proportions signal that they're different. Their attractive size suggests they contain something special and powerful. This is confirmed by the bold product names that promote damson, quince and gooseberry – fruits from a past era, with beautiful poetic names, that are now experiencing a culinary renaissance.

The striking sorbet-coloured labels, with compartmentalized layouts defined by fine keylines, and confection of typefaces including the blocky slab-serifed name, look almost nineteenth century in style. However, their fashionable colour palette and contemporary verbal language make them modern. The sumptuous ripe-fruit-coloured letters of the damson pack are placed on a pale blue background that conjures up images of the dark fruit with its pale velvet sheen. The green of the gooseberry label looks sharp and tart, while the orangey-red of quince suggests the vivid amber hue of the purée.

05

Pack   **The Fine Cheese Co.**
               Mustard & Black Pepper
               Oat Digestives
Client   **The Fine Cheese Co., UK**
Designer **Julian Roberts,**
               Irving Designs, UK
Year   **2006**

The Fine Cheese Co. has leveraged its reputation for speciality cheeses, and its premium identity and packaging, to extend the range of products it offers and grow its brand. Its diverse foods and beverages, including conserves, biscuits and wines, are selected for their compatibility with cheese and packaged to promote the company's gastronomic ideology.

Mustard & Black Pepper Oat Digestives for Mature Cheddar is one variety in a range of oat biscuits that use their packaging to promote the company's brand and communicate a handcrafted, wholesome, natural-looking product that's intended to be eaten with cheese. The uncoated and textured, slightly off-white, card carton evokes the handmade texture and natural appearance of the biscuits. Charmingly naive hand-drawn illustrations and typography, including depictions of pepper mills, cheeses and biscuits, are used to describe the ingredients. A decorative patterned border of oat grass runs around the product name and up the sides of the carton, dividing it into four panels and adding value by giving the appearance of a quaint, old-fashioned box.

The softness of the brown and yellow colour palette, and the textured patterns, evoke the crumbliness of mature cheese and the crispiness of the biscuits. A little gentle humour is added by endearing drawings of peppercorns and mustard grains.

01   Keane, *Under the Iron Sea*, 12" LP cover, inner cover and vinyl record. Sanna Annukka's iconic illustration style is used to link different parts of the same pack and each of the different products that compose the album and its promotion.

02   *Under the Iron Sea*, CD. The core illustration used to promote the album is featured on the CD pack.

02

Case Study
'Under the Iron Sea' album and book

Pack	***Under the Iron Sea*** **album and book**
Client	**Keane, UK**
	Record label: Island
Designer	**Art direction: Richard Andrews and Gerard Saint, Big Active**
	Design: Richard Andrews, Big Active, UK
	Illustrations: Sanna Annukka
Year	**2006**

The music industry uses design to create some of the world's most beautiful and covetable packs. Because music is intangible, packaging design is vital in expressing the character of the product and giving it a unique visual appearance that allows it to be effectively promoted and sold.

Keane are a hugely successful band signed to the Island recording label. After the international success of their first album they wanted to adopt an intuitive and symbolic approach to the design of their second one. In order to do this they collaborated with Big Active, who introduced the band to Sanna Annukka and her iconic illustrative style. Her distinctive graphic prints helped the designers to create a monolithic and recognizable album-based campaign, and a design solution that could be applied to the subsequent release of singles and throughout a wide range of associated promotional media, including marketing and advertising.

The pack features a roll-folded booklet that opens on its side to reveal a long, dark, fairytale-like illustration. The image expresses the lyrical content and emotional character of Keane's songs, such as 'Atlantic', and also promotes a distinctive and memorable identity, centred around the album, for the entire campaign.

As the image unfolds, panel by panel, it draws the viewer deeper down into a dark, congested, claustrophobic and chaotic world beneath the waves where decapitated soldiers haemorrhage orange blood. This beautiful but disturbing image describes the album's sinister mood, expressed in tracks with titles such as 'A Bad Dream' and 'Broken Toy'.

When it was released, *Under the Iron Sea* went straight to number one in the United Kingdom's album chart, and debuted at number four in the United States Billboard chart before selling over 2.5 million copies worldwide.

Interview with Gerard Saint, *Creative Director, Big Active*

What was the context for this project?
Keane were eager to adopt an intuitive design approach for their second album. The band had been introduced to Sanna Annukka's illustrative work and they liked her distinctive graphic approach.

Jon Turner, from the band's record label, Island, felt we should art direct the project to produce a robust design solution that could work at all levels. We'd been looking for an opportunity to collaborate with Sanna, so this seemed like a really good fit.

Does packaging music have particular design challenges?
Music design is about having an intuitive relationship with the band and the campaign. It's about creating energy around a release. A campaign of this scale is always going to be highly visible internationally, so it's important that the design is focused. Sanna's imagery gives the overall project a distinctive flavour that embraces the feeling behind the music.

01　　　　*Is It Any Wonder*, 7"
record cover and vinyl record. While
the same illustration style is used
throughout the album the colour
palette is varied to differentiate single
tracks featured on 7" vinyl records.

02　　　　*Nothing In My Way*, 7" record
cover and vinyl record. A blue colour
palette is used to link various products
that feature as part of the whole album.

01

02

03　　A Bad Dream, 7" record cover and vinyl record. A red colour palette is used to express the hellish nightmare theme and lyrics of this track.

04　　Crystal Ball, 7" record cover and vinyl record. Sanna Annukka's particular stencil-like illustration style was chosen because it suited the style of the music. It helps to promote the album by being strongly individualistic and therefore recognizable in the marketplace.

03

04

01   Cover detail of Keane's *Under the Iron Sea* limited edition book and DVD. Colour and typography link this limited edition book with the other items that are part of the album release. The sea theme is also expressed through the wave-like ornaments that form part of the letter 'A'.

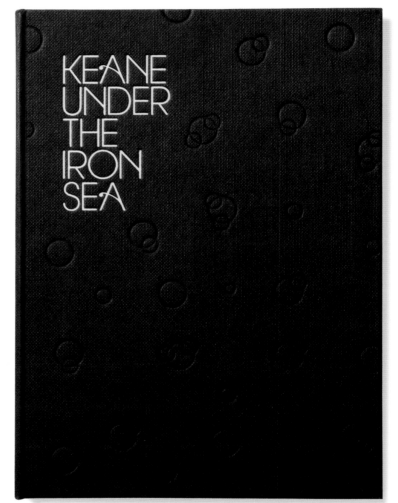

01

What did the project involve?
A defining image that works for the album and related singles, advertising, marketing materials and promotion.
     The band have built an international reputation, so it's important that there is strong visual cohesion between the elements. The first task was to find a visual solution for the album and work outwards from there.
     The band were interested in bringing together symbols that underscored the ideas behind their songs. Taking our inspiration from Picasso's wartime *Guernica* we

fused the visual claustrophobia of the painting with ominous fairytale references suited to, and counteracted by, Sanna's 'innocent' style and delivered a visual twist. We created a long panel-like image that forms the 'bigger picture' within the album and then selected elements from it to use in the singles.

What was the process?
We asked Sanna to interpret the lyrics and create images and moods to kick-start the collaborative process, and produce elements for the bigger picture theme in the

album interior. We realized that the 'other world' might be something submerged under a figurative surface – the deeper you fell the more impenetrable it became – leading to the CD being in a roll-folded booklet inserted sideways to make a downwards fold, producing a vertical panel image for the bigger picture that created a sense of depth. The album cover symbolizes a tormented sea. We created a limited colour palette to differentiate each release. Richard developed typography that could be used also for titles and headline copy,

02   Interior spread from *Under the Iron Sea* limited edition book and DVD. Sanna Annukka has also illustrated a children's storybook-styled book designed to add a collectable dimension to the album and its promotion.

02

creating a strong identity even when no imagery is used.

Were there any technical challenges?
This is a major worldwide release and the packaging formats reflect this. The band were eager to achieve a tactile result that suited the imagery. So we specified uncoated papers. We also created a limited edition album, including a DVD of live material and videos by directors including Kevin Godley and Irving Welsh, in an illustrated hardback storybook format that contains illustrated lyrics.

The album imagery was reinterpreted to create a range for ambient media including street advertising and billboards, and a moving window display for Virgin Megastore in London's Oxford Street.

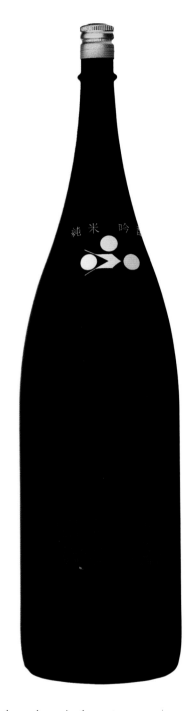

07

Pack   **Fukunishiki sake**
Client   **Fukunishiki Company,**
          Japan
Designer **Graph, Japan**
Year   **2005**

This handsome branded pack helps Fukunishiki to promote its premium Japanese sake to a new generation of consumers while also honouring and retaining its traditional but ageing customer base.

Fukunishiki's visual identity is designed by Issay Kitagawa, whose motto is 'reduce to the max'. He has used his extensive knowledge of Japanese printing traditions and new technologies to rebrand and package the 200-year-old distillery's range of products.

The pack's monochrome label emphasizes the subtle textural contrasts between paper, glass and foil, acknowledging Japanese graphic tradition and communicating a sophisticated and crafted pack and product.

The logo, shown in the centre of the label, is a pictogram of a grain of rice, as well as of the letter 'fu', suggesting the company's name. Visual, verbal and cultural connotations maintain the distillery's links with tradition, but more elaborate versions no longer work because old relationships between everyday things – like rice and sake – have been forgotten.

The enigmatic bottle teases the customer by obscuring the product while also reassuring them of its high quality. This is reaffirmed by the champagne-style foil covering the metal screw enclosure, which adds value and drama as the pack is unwrapped. The outer carton extends the experience and transforms the product into a gift.

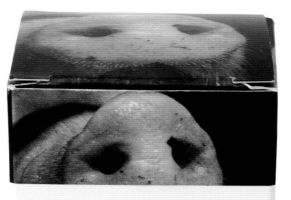

HARVEY NICHOLS

WHITE TRUFFLE
& MUSHROOM
SAUCE

net wt 80g e

08

Pack   Harvey Nichols White
              Truffle & Mushroom
              Sauce
Client   Harvey Nichols, UK
Designer   Michael Nash
              Associates, UK
Year   2002

Harvey Nichols has created a systematic approach to its packaging design that allows it to apply its premium brand consistently across a variety of different products without undermining its fashion business or compromising the gourmet credentials of its foods.

This allows the company to accommodate different-sized bottles, boxes, bags and tins, made from different materials, within a single Harvey Nichols brand, made recognizable by white label-like banding, classic centred typography, a limited colour palette and consistent compositional style. Duotone photography (half-tone images composed of two colours) is used to provide flexibility and allows each pack to be tailored to reflect some aspect of its product. This ensures packs are not unduly constrained by a boring and repetitive one-size-fits-all formula solution, and provides customers with a memorable and emotional touchstone that makes them feel positive about the products. The duotone photographs also communicate their narrative meaning more forcefully than if they were in colour, which would divert the viewer's attention from the dramatic action and essence of the images.

09

Pack   *The Journal
            of Popular Noise*
Client   **Byron Kalet,
            Popular Noise, USA**
Designer   **Byron Kalet,
            Popular Noise, USA**
Year   **2008**

The Journal of Popular Noise is a semi-annual audio magazine that promotes its iconoclastic identity to its niche customers through the design of its packaging.

The journal's publisher, Byron Kalet, is also its designer, and a musician who is fascinated by the relationship between the senses of sight and of sound and the qualities they have in common, such as composition and rhythm.

The demise of the vinyl album and its 12 inch graphic artwork reduced the opportunities for some new graphic designers to hone their skills, and this was the source of inspiration for the creation of this new hybrid format designed to put graphic design back into music packaging.

Each issue of the journal mixes the formal conventions of publication design with those of the vinyl record sleeve to create a magazine that is also a package containing three 7 inch vinyl records produced by a different band or artist.

All the issues follow the same editorial and design formula based on a set of instructions and a diagram that are sent to the band or group. The whole pack is assembled from a single folded sheet of inexpensive Mohawk superfine paper, printed by letterpress (because the visceral, old-fashion technology mimics the physical, analogue quality of the vinyl records) and produced in a signed and numbered limited edition.

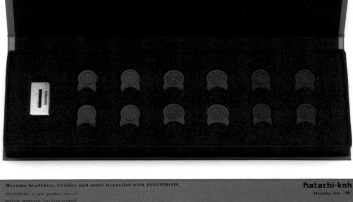

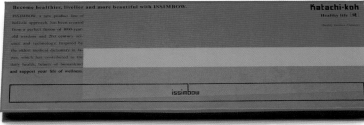

10

Pack   **Issimbow incense**
Client   **Issimbow, Japan**
Designer   **Shin Matsunaga**
           Design, Japan
Year   **2006**

The name, Issimbow, is based on the *Ishinhou*, a 1,000-year-old Japanese medical compendium, and the ideas are combined with twenty-first-century science and technology to create this beautiful and colourful incense, or Katachi-Koh, brand and pack.

Issimbow promotes the idea of a healthier, more beautiful, more energetic life through its concept of wellness and reducing stress. Through collaboration with ideologically similar companies, Issimbow aims to expand its product range and develop new brands that will promote their refreshing ethos, and continue their success both domestically and internationally. Issimbow's range of incense is based on Chinese herbal medicines, curative ingredients and modern components associated with physical and mental energy. The incense is shaped into solid cakes, inspired by traditional forms, which are burnt to release their fragrances.

While product packaging is the foundation of this brand, colour is its most powerful element. Sumptuous geometrical compositions promote the beautiful and healthy brand essence by being both visually sumptuous and emotionally uplifting.

The decorative presentation-style card box reinforces the preciousness of the product, which is displayed on sober black, dramatically contrasting the pack's exterior and interior. The ordered rows of incense imply a ritual course of treatment that references the medicinal history and ancient traditions of incense while also being totally, beautifully, modern.

11

Pack   **Maroma Encens
           d'Auroville**
Client   **Maroma, India**
Designer   **Design: André
           Hababou
           Typography: Vajya,
           India**
Year   **2007**

Maroma's incense business was founded in Auroville in India in 1976, when its range of 12 fragrances generated economic activity in an experimental new town constructed by 1,500 people from 30 different countries. The company has a sustainable ideology and supports education and health initiatives, and tsunami-relief work.

Through its branded packaging these little envelopes promote Maroma's incense products and support its socioeconomic projects. The packaging is a vital physical manifestation of the brand and has a different personality on each face. The envelope front describes both the organization's 1970s origins and the product's smoky characteristics, also evoked by the handwritten typeface and fluid composition. The reverse is a modern, structured design based on Mogul art in the Taj Mahal.

The development of the product and the pack design ran concurrently and took approximately one year to complete. A key element of the pack and the brand is the locally made paper handcrafted from recycled cotton fibres, which characterizes the organization's ethos and expresses its handmade qualities.

Today, there are 50 fragrances in Maroma's Encens d'Auroville Incense range and 15 product lines, including candles and bodycare products. These are distributed in 19 countries worldwide and the income they generate helps to promote and sustain the Auroville community.

01   Voya Lazy Days seaweed
bath. This pack uses natural craft card
and swaying seaweed to promote
its organic seaweed contents.

02   Voya Rub A Dub Dub
soap. Different sections of Wendy
Kavanagh's seaweed illustration
are used to help differentiate each
pack and link the whole range.

02

Case Study
Voya bath and body range

Pack   Voya bath and
            body range
Client   Voya, Ireland
Designer   Wendy Kavanagh,
            Dynamo Design
            Consultants, UK
Year   2007

It took Voya six years to research and produce the world's first range of certified organic seaweed-based cosmetics. By doing this the company transformed common, low-value plants into precious natural products whose value has been consolidated through the design of their distinctive packaging. By developing branding and packaging centred on seaweed Voya has created a unique identity in the international cosmetics and skincare sector.

The packaging of Voya's bath and body products expresses the brand's natural, organic, botanical and lyrical qualities. While the brand has its origins in the wild and picturesque Atlantic coast of Ireland, and its name (derived from 'voyage') may perhaps be interpreted as being Irish, it is conceived as a premium international brand for customers seeking natural organic products produced in harmony with nature.

Despite the challenges of designing a premium spa brand based on 'weeds', the result is distinctive, beautiful and robust. The brand is consistently and systematically applied to a range of items including card boxes, plastic tubes and glass bottles, using just one illustration of a strand of seaweed and one typeface. The only other colours used in addition to black and white are a fresh yellowy-green and brown. Many of the packs also feature brown kraft board that evokes the natural texture and organic quality of the seaweed.

The seaweed contained in many of the products is alive and reactivates when it is reintroduced to water – a characteristic expressed by the dynamic, floating style of the drawings.

Another element in the packaging and branding is the verbal identities of the products. Names like Lazy Days, Rub a Dub Dub and Softly Does It suggest languorous, playful and relaxing experiences, and, along with the carefully crafted typography, help to civilize a wild product and transport it from the sea to the spa.

Interview with Wendy Kavanagh, Designer, Dynamo Design Consultants

Was it hard to design a pack for a brand that's centred around seaweed?
I didn't feel restricted by the seaweed at all.

How did you create the floating seaweed image?
It's an illustration. I hand-drew the outline shape and then used Photoshop for the watery effect, using the airbrush tool. It took me a day and a half to do and it became the main symbol for the brand. It's used again and again, and what I do is I cut into it and crop it to wrap around the different box designs I have to work with, because obviously all the boxes aren't the same and the seaweed doesn't always work so I have to make it work.

Why did you choose the particular shade of yellowy-green for the packs?
We chose green because the product is organic. A lot of the products are endorsed by the Soil Association, so green was a natural choice. And then the brown is obviously the seaweed.

01   Voya plastic and card packs.
A brown and vibrant green colour palette
expresses the natural and organic
qualities of these plant-based products.

01

And we always wanted a brown-paper effect because we felt that brown paper communicated the idea of organic.

Does the paper have environmental credentials?
It's recyclable and we have a travel set that is the first product printed on recycled board. The aim as time goes on is to have everything printed on fully recycled materials.

Are the plastic and glass packs bespoke or off-the-shelf?
They are standard off the shelf packs but we did get to choose them.

Are they recycled or recyclable?
Glass was chosen because it's reusable. The plastic – at the moment it's not recyclable. But in the future our client is hoping to source recyclable plastic.

What is the typeface?
It's Gotham. It's used on all collateral – there isn't a secondary typeface, just Gotham. It's a really versatile font and I love the rounded nature of the letters, and it squares off very well. And if you blow it up in size it sets beautifully.

Did it take you long to develop the design approach to the packs?
We started in November 2005 and the first boxes went on sale the following year – it took eight to 12 months to get the first products on the shelf. Since then we've been producing a product every three to four months.

Did you do any testing?
We didn't do any testing but Voya did.

Did you get client feedback?
Absolutely, constantly, yes! They are a fantastic client to work with. They always

02   Voya teas. Painstakingly crafted compositions, one typeface and single-colour silhouetted illustrations of plants and flowers contribute to the high quality of these minimalist packs.

02

try their hardest to get the most premium stock and foils – whatever we ask for they always try their best.

Did you develop the verbal element of the brand?
The first one we came up with was Lazy Days, and then Softly Does It. I usually come up with them on the way into work on the bus! Other people do feed into the process along the way.

13

Pack   **Kevin Murphy Homme
           haircare range**
Client   **Kevin Murphy, Australia**
Designer   **Kevin Murphy, Australia**
Year   **2003**

This range of packaging promotes the iconoclastic ethos of its creator, celebrity hair stylist and innovator Kevin Murphy. His simple haircare philosophy – 'strength, moisture and regeneration' – is delivered by his extraordinary product range, which is literally a series of '"building blocks" to great hair'.

The decorative card outer carton was originally conceived as a secular 'Christmas' gift pack that could also be used to celebrate special holidays anywhere in the world.

The axonometric illustration of the products contained within it, and its extra-large silver-foiled sans serif type, have an industrial aesthetic that reveals Kevin Murphy's interest in mechanical design, perspective drawings, Japanese design and simplicity in all things.

Each of the distinctive injection-moulded polypropylene inner packs took two years and around 12 prototypes to develop. They were evolved alongside the products in order to create a total solution where product, pack, information, seal and enclosure are perfectly integrated in one single, unified design that is focused on promoting and adding value to the brand.

The deceptively simple matt coloured jerrycan packs are elevated on tiny feet that keep them dry if they are placed on a wet surface and also create a shadow gap that makes them appear to float on the shelf.

14

Pack   Korres Marigold & Ginseng
          Aftershave Balm
Client   Korres Natural Products,
          Greece
Designer   Structural design:
          Helene Prablanc,
          Korres Natural Products
          Graphic design: K2 Design,
          Greece
Year   2007

Capitalizing on its herbalist roots, which can be traced back to the first homeopathic pharmacy in Athens, Korres has developed 500 innovative, botanically derived skin, hair and sun care products including nutraceuticals cosmetics and a herbal-pharmacy range.

This unusual pack from the Korres Men's Line uses the company's instantly recognizable graphic labelling to promote its core brand. This is typified by a sumptuous colour palette, a structured modern layout style with thick keylines, sans serif type set in capital letters and beautiful, strongly abstract close-up photography of botanical ingredients. However, the Men's Line products are differentiated from other Korres lines by their striking polypropylene containers with asymmetrical caps and actuators, and bespoke rich brown colouring.

Black features prominently within the label, cap and outer packs, and is used to link all the products in Korres' Men's Line. It also appears on the 100 per cent recyclable card outer carton, where its use as a background colour expresses the masculinity of the product type (or 'edition') and contrasts perfectly with the saturated colours in the photographs.

By seamlessly integrating its graphic brand through all its media, including product packaging, retail interiors and marketing collateral, today Korres operates successfully in 30 countries.

Pack **Leitz Weingut**
Client **Leitz Weingut, German**
Designer **Fuenfwerken, Germany**
Year **2007**

Johannes Leitz, a radical winemaker whose wines are clean and to the point, worked closely with the designers throughout the eight-week project to create product packaging for his winery. The result is a beautiful and distinctive range of bottles and cartons that promotes the Leitz brand throughout every aspect of the winery's operations – from its building signage and products to its packaging and online presence.

Leitz' minimal design is unique compared to those of other German winemakers because, despite recent technological innovations in wine production, the majority of producers continue to promote their products using traditionally styled packaging such as gold-foiled medieval 'black face' typography, stylized wine leaves or watercolour illustrations of landscapes.

While packaging is used to distinguish Leitz as an overtly modern wine grower, the winery's heritage and its regional provenance are acknowledged in the design. The tripartite colour palette represents the three factors that impact on the flavour of the wine: the dark and wide Rhine River that influences the climate; the sunlight reflecting from its surface, which gives the vines their vigour; and the meagre soil that gives the grapes their characteristic taste.

The bespoke typography also evokes the business's historical and Germanic roots, but it, too, appears fresh, clean and contemporary.

01   Xocoa's retail interior. Xocoa's
colourful patterned packs provide the retail
decoration and promote the product.

02   Each Xocoa chocolate
uses type and decoration to promote
a different flavour or variety.

02

Case Study
Xocoa
chocolate bars

16

Pack   Xocoa chocolate bars
Client   Xocoa, Spain
Designer   Mucho, Spain
Year   2007

The Escursell brothers, disc jockey Marc and chocolatier Miguel, have breathed new life into their family pâtisserie business by commissioning Mucho to create a new identity and packaging for a vibrant range of chocolate bars and boxes.

The brothers are obsessed with chocolate and packaging in equal measure. Their youthful brand is focused on their unique combination of graphic design and chocolate, which has created an energetic and diverse range of wrappers, boxes and bags that take their inspiration from music and nightclubs.

Mucho's simple and robust identity system is centred on the chocolate bar. The logotype is a diagonal lozenge depicting four squares of chocolate with the company's name placed at the same angle. To help to promote the Xocoa brand it is systematically applied to each product wrapper where, together with a single-coloured band, it performs as a simple container for graphic contributions from different designers. This straightforward but flexible system means the wrapper design can vary while still being a recognizable part of the brand. A diverse range of different packs can be branded to promote the products, the graphic artists who design the wrappers, and the company – simultaneously creating a covetable visual feast of gourmet chocolate. By applying the brand to other products that benefit from this graphic approach and fit Xocoa's philosophy, including candles, clothing and music CDs, the business has quickly grown and diversified.

Like Andy Warhol's Pop Art prints of Campbell's soup cans, the chocolate bars are displayed in multiples to heighten the visual impact of their vivid patterns, colours and typography. This lavish graphic banquet dominates a shop, and extends the packaging design into the retail environment – which also functions as a supersized product display – transforming it into an art gallery whose single aim is to promote Xocoa chocolate.

Interview with Pablo Juncadella,
Designer and Art Director, Mucho

What was the context for the project?
Xocoa is owned by two brothers – a pâtissier who makes cakes and chocolates, and a disc jockey. They came to us to rebrand their chocolate company and do something quite different. Instead of creating a fixed corporate identity we established a direction, and a common language.

The project was always more about art directing a brand than just giving the client a design and letting them deal with it.

How did you develop the brief?
We sit down with them. They want to launch a new kind of chocolate or a new way of eating chocolate, so we think of ideas and consider how much product will be produced – because this often defines what we can do. Then we create a graphic language that will talk about that product. And we present it to them and they give us their thoughts. We work along with them. Ideas can come from both the designers and the clients.

01   Xocoa Limón chocolate bar. A citrus-inspired colour palette and repeat lemon tree flower motif promote the flavour of this chocolate.

02   Xocoa Wasabi chocolate bar. A green coloured Yin and Yang symbol promotes the flavour while a systematic approach to composition promotes the whole range of chocolate bars.

03   Xocoa Chili chocolate bar. Fire is used to instantly communicate the distinguishing ingredient in this pack.

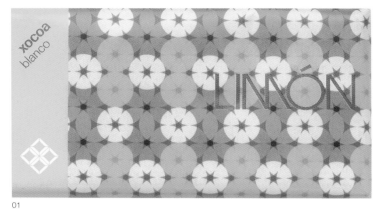
01

02

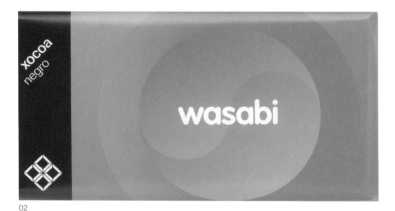
03

Does Xocoa's brand express multiple personalities?
Chocolate by definition is fun. Those products that are really fun – we make them appear funny. And those that are very serious – they have to be serious too. The graphics needed to show that difference – between the feeling you have in a supermarket and the feeling you have in an Armani shop.

What is the relationship between Xocoa's brand and its packaging?
One of the difficult things about this project was that because we didn't go for one colour and one way of doing things the clients came to a point where they thought 'Why don't we get these guys for that pack or those guys to do another pack?'. And after a while they found out that they needed someone who had a general view, and decided to work with us providing general direction.

The boundaries are not straightforward – these are not the sort of graphics you can explain in a corporate identity manual.

Does the packaging influence the retail environment?
Yes. The packaging has a big role to play. Every product is an advertisement for itself. When you see it in the shop it stands out on its own and catches the attention of whoever's there to buy it. After looking at four different boxes all with the same shape, colour and all that, you stop looking – you concentrate on the things that stand out. In retail there's always a neutral background with different products showing their different characteristics.

04   Xocoa Té Verde chocolate bar. Because each bar of chocolate has a different colour palette and composition the chocolate bars, when displayed together in the shop, form a cohesive range.

05   Xocoa Chocolate de Yoghourt con Fresitas del Bosque chocolate bar. A soft, milky typeface is used to express the yoghurt content of this bar.

04

05

Who is the target market?
Chocolate is for everybody and the public likes very different kinds – from white chocolate to dark. Dark chocolate is quite a refined thing. White chocolate is for kids. So we created a common ground, a graphic universe that talks to different people in different ways. There's a common language that embraces the individual language of each pack.

17

Pack	Monokuro Boo character
Client	San-X Company, Japan
Designer	San-X Company, Japan
Year	2005

An anonymous female employee of the San-X Company in Japan created the two popular black-and-white piggy characters that appear on this pack, and on many other packs and products. Here, the logo (left) is shown on a mobile phone strap (right, 2006).

Monokuro is the Japanese word for monochromatic, and *Boo* is the onomatopoeic word for oink – the sound made by a pig. The cartoon characters are licensed to businesses worldwide who feature them in products and services, or apply them to packaging, in order to sell goods ranging from cellphone wallpaper to pencils and *bento* (Japanese lunch boxes).

Cartoon characters enable brands to distinguish their branded products and services in the marketplace and give generic products vital characterization, adding to their value and allowing them to be promoted to new customers and markets.

The wide range of popular cartoon characters available provides limitless opportunities for businesses to repackage, differentiate and promote their existing output by associating it with one that helps them to develop new markets or extend the life of waning products and services.

This mobile phone strap pack demonstrates how the Monokuro Boo character is used to extend the manufacturer's existing product line and customer base. By leveraging the brand loyalty associated with a cartoon the packaging has become more valuable than the product.

Pack   REN Moroccan Rose
           Otto Bath Oil
Client   REN, UK
Designer   John Perlmutter and
           Dwayne Lewars,
           Earth Design, UK
Year   2007

REN's skincare products are founded on the company's five principles: Right Ingredients, Right Science, Right Product Experience, Right Environmental Impact and Right Attitude. These principles are promoted through the design of their packaging to communicate their systematic and systemic brand, which represents the total product from formulation and customer experience to product efficacy.

The company uses a utilitarian pharmaceutical-style glass bottle with a white plastic lid and white label to promote the product's scientific principles. Glass does not taint the oil and is heavy, therefore communicating high quality.

The transparent container also expresses the clear environmental principles embedded in the product while the lightweight typography characterizes its delicate natural ingredients.

The star flower is an amalgamation of star qualities; scientific-looking cell structures, natural botanical references and beautiful blooms that communicate the brand's ideology in visual shorthand.

REN's crisp white label and outer carton are tempered by a fashionable tonal colour palette that makes the pack fashionable rather than functional. The spare, undecorated composition looks underdesigned and signals eco-awareness while also

focusing attention on the lyrical names of the ingredients.

The sober white card outer boxes open like the petals of a flower and burst into colourful patterned life – perfectly promoting REN's bioactive personality.

19

Pack   **Saks Fifth Avenue**
            packaging
Client   **Saks Fifth Avenue, USA**
Designer   **Michael Bierut,**
            Pentagram Design, USA
Year   **2007**

Opened in 1924, Saks Fifth Avenue has a distinguished history as a speciality store that is synonymous with fashionable living and premium brands. This quintessential New York institution promotes its 'unmistakably Saks' brand through its signature carrier bags and boxes, which add value to its products and services and confer status on its customers.

The packaging is derived from a new logotype based on what has been Saks's calligraphic identity for more than 50 years. The logotype is divided into sections that are rearranged to create a bold, black-and-white pattern featuring details of the store's iconic typography. Each section reminds customers of Saks's famous logotype with its 'fancy lettering'. This branded pattern can be applied to packaging whose purpose is to unify, and own, a wide variety of items by enveloping them in the Saks brand.

The calligraphic monochrome pattern is both recognizable and visible, and has the advantage of being used to contain, and add value to, other brands sold in the store. This means the Saks brand gains value by packaging, and being associated with, some of the world's most valuable brands, and bestows value on tomorrow's emerging premium brands – making it a useful and very valuable commodity.

When brands exist over generations they transcend commerce and become part of culture. Saks is not only a New York institution, it is also an internationally recognized retailer. Designers must therefore respect the many different constituencies that have a relationship with these iconic establishments and ensure they remain attractive and recognizable to those who know them. They must tread carefully when designing a new manifestation of a very old brand – after all, if something's not broken, don't mend it or replace it. This signature-like commercial style of script, typeset in three lines to create a balanced composition, is placed within a square box, thereby increasing the size of the logotype and separating it from any coloured or patterned background. This has the effect of making the logotype more prominent and legible, and making it look like a label that can be applied to products and packaging. Pentagram extended the label idea into the design of packaging, including boxes and bags.

20

Pack   **Selfridges & Co**
            own-brand goods
Client   **Selfridges, UK**
Designer   **R Design, UK**
Year   **2007**

Selfridges is one of the United Kingdom's most famous department stores. Founded in 1909, it has the reputation of being one of the world's most fashionable and innovative retailers.

As well as selling many different brands, Selfridges has leveraged its world-class name by promoting its range of premium-quality own-brand foods. To distinguish its products from those of other manufacturers, they are packaged according to the same one-size-fits-all branded system. Foods ranging from crisps and champagne to tea and biscuits adopt the same consistent and systematic approach centred on a common black background, the Trade Gothic typeface in one point size, and one style of composition. A contrasting palette of jewel-like highlight colours is used to differentiate the products and express the characteristics of their contents.

By 'owning' the colour black, Selfridges' glossy and matt bottles, jars, packets and boxes contrast with their branded competitors and stand out on the shelves like dark punctuation points. Their unremittingly modern approach also has the effect of modernizing old-fashioned products such as champagne. Like the archetypal little black dress, the distinctive packs are both the epitome of classic style and a simple and effective way to consolidate, extend and promote its brand.

21

Pack | Paul Smith
| Extreme perfume
Client | Paul Smith, UK
Designer | Alan Aboud,
| Aboud Creative, UK
Year | 2002

At the start of the new millennium Paul Smith wanted to create a new limited edition perfume that would invigorate its brand but would not generate a second fragrance line.

Aboud Creative had already designed Paul Smith's iconic stripe, and the swirl pattern used in the company's branded communications but not in its products or packaging. However, the perfume licensee, Inter Parfums, recognized the potential for striped packaging and, as the perfume was a limited edition, persuaded the company to deviate from using the standard logotype.

The stripes are applied to the glass bottle by dye sublimation – similar to an iron-on transfer – and the bottle is then 'cooked' and the colour is fused to the glass. Dye sublimation is usually restricted to six colours, and as the Paul Smith stripes contained 38, the original design was modified – further expressing the idea of a limited edition.

Rather than simply applying the Paul Smith logotype, the signature is etched on to the bottle after the stripes have been applied. Paul Smith experimented with a variety of pens to re-create his own signature on the side of the bottle, accompanied by the handwritten word 'extreme'. The perfume sold out immediately and is now the company's second fragrance line!

22

Pack   **Anthony's Super brandies**
Client   **Anthony's Mini Garage**
         Winery, Germany
Designer   **Kolle & Rebbe, Germany**
Year   **2007**

These fruit brandies are targeted at premium bar-restaurants and are designed to be displayed on the bar. The unusual name, fashionable graphics and specially designed 'Edelstahl' (stainless-steel) screw-topped cans contrast strongly with competitors' glass containers to create a distinctive range of desirable and attractive packs.

Anthony Hammond first produced his brandies in a former garage, and their unique origin inspired the motor vehicle-style of the cans, which look like containers for industrial oil or lubricants.

Anthony's Super hip flask-style canisters for schnapps suit the current trend for portable 'label drinking', where products are consumed on the move (and often on the dance floor) and directly from their containers. In this context the packs, unlike glass, are safe and unbreakable. They are also powerful components in Anthony's visual identity. In this way they promote the brand and confer status on the consumer.

The graphic illustrations are modern interpretations of Art Nouveau and Jugendstil floral decoration, made contemporary by being rendered in silhouette using a minimalist, monochrome, metallic colour palette. They contrast with the bold industrial sans serif type where P stands for plum brandy, C for cherry brandy and W for brandy made from Williams pears.

23

Pack   **Alessi**
Client   **Alessi, Italy**
Designer **Alessi, Italy**
Year   **2008**

Alessi is famous for its homeware and accessories, created by some of the world's best-known architects and designers.

The company uses packaging to promote and add more prestige to its already valuable products by providing a bespoke packaging service.

Alessi invites customers to select products, then choose packaging from a menu of different types of pack. Options include a range of plain-coloured card boxes available in standard sizes, bespoke wooden boxes, or colourful cutlery trays with matching coloured cloth bags. Card presentation boxes have die-cut card or vacuum-formed plastic inner trays to hold products securely in place and prevent them

being damaged during transit. Each inner box has a decorative printed pattern that contextualizes the products. For example, the pack containing a cocktail shaker and bar tools features a background pattern of playing cards to evoke a sophisticated nightclub or casino environment.

When customers have chosen their pack they can select the colour and content of a customized external paper band that wraps around the box and secures it. The band is printed in a single colour that coordinates with the box and includes silhouette-style icons that describe the items contained within. Written messages or corporate logotypes can also be included.

Project credits

Alcor
Pati Núñez, Esther Martin –
    Pati Núñez Associats
Kimberly Hanzich –
    The Art Directors Club
www.patinunez.com
www.adcglobal.org
Alessi
Pete Collard – Weir Willats Associates
www.alessi.com
Alphabet
Shoko Hamomoto, Suzuki Motohiro,
    Yukiko Seto – Japan
    Tobacco International
Chris Pettit – Gallaher Group
www.jti.com
www.asyl.co.jp
www.gallaher-group.com
Andres Sarda Lingerie
Eugene Lagache, Pablo Juncadella – Mucho
www.andressarda.com
www.mucho.ws
Anthony's Super
Simone – Anthony's Garage Winery
Thomas Stritz, Kristna Wulf –
    Kolle & Rebbe
www.garagewinery.de
www.korefe.de
Apple MacBook Pro and iPod Nano
Jonathan Ive, Susan Lundgren,
    Sue Carroll – Apple USA
www.apple.com
Arroz Sivaris
Baptiste Pons – Pepe Gimeno
www.sivaris.eu
www.pepegimeno.net
Basi Homme and Basi Femme
Armand Basi
Pati Núñez, Esther Martin –
    Pati Núñez Associats
Kimberly Hanzich –
    The Art Directors Club
www.armandbasi.com
www.patinunez.com
www.adcglobal.org

BP LPG Gas Light
Craig Stoddart – BP LPG
Ragasco
www.bp.com
Camper
Martí Guixé
Inga Knolke – ImageKontainer
www.camper.com
www.imagekontainer.com
www.guixe.com
Caol Ila® Aged 23 Years
Lucy Pritchard, Sarah Ogilvie – Diageo
Stuart Graham – Sedley Place
www.diageo.com
www.sedley-place.com
www.whisky-distilleries.info
Chocolate Abyss
Gary McGann, David Craig –
    Espresso Warehouse
www.espressowarehouse.com
www.graven.co.uk
Chocolates Rohr
Roger Rohr – Rohr Chocolate Maison
www.chocolats-rohr.ch
Chocovic Cobertus Selváticas
Pati Núñez, Esther Martin –
    Pati Núñez Associats
Kimberly Hanzich –
    The Art Directors Club
www.chocovic.es
www.patinunez.com
www.adcglobal.org
Cohiba Minis
Enrique Babot – Habanos
Sean Croley – Hunters & Frankau
Jan Nimmo
www.habanos.com
www.cigars.co.uk
Comme des Garçons Series 1, 5 and 6
Anne-Sophie Marquetty, Annika
    McVeigh – Comme des Garçons
www.guerrilla-store.com

Demasié
Eugene Lagache, Pablo Juncadella –
    Mucho
www.demasie.es
www.mucho.ws
Deutche See Fisch-Box
Jessica Wilckens –
    Feldmann + Schultchen
www.fsdesign.de
Dr. Bronner's Magic Soaps
Lisa Milam – Dr Bronner's
www.drbronner.com
Dylon Cold Water Dye
Sophie Cotgrove – Dylon
www.dylon.co.uk
Ecopod
Hazel Selina, Peter Rock – Ecopod
www.ecopod.co.uk
Effol Hufsalbe
Silke Schawe, Stefanie Brüffer
www.effax.de
Equerry
Stacey Coates – Vale Brothers
www.valebrothers.co.uk
Espa
Domenic Lippa, Simon Beresford-Smith –
    Pentagram Design, UK
www.espainternational.co.uk
www.pentagram.com
Essenz
Gary McGann – Espresso Warehouse
www.espressowarehouse.com
www.graven.co.uk
Established & Sons
Ben Parker, Paul Austin, Eve Skillicorn –
    MadeThought
www.establishedandsons.com
www.madethought.com
EverEdgeIP CrushPak
Eddie Szopa, Andrew Smith – Fonterra
Paul Adams, Bradley Mitchell –
    EverEdgeIP
www.fonterra.com
www.everedgeip.com

Fee Brothers Bitters
Joe Fee, Donna Colucci – Fee Brothers
Andrew Weir – Coe Vintners
www.feebrothers.com
www.coevintners.com
The Fine Cheese Co.
Fruits and Digestives
Flo Ahlers, Ann-Marie Dyas –
    The Fine Cheese Co.
Julian Roberts – Irving Designs
www.finecheese.co.uk
www.irvingdesigns.com
The Food Doctor
Rosie Buckler, Dave Richmond –
    R Design
www.thefooddoctor.com
www.r-design.co.uk
Fuensanta
Pati Núñez, Esther Martin –
    Pati Núñez Associats
Kimberly Hanzich –
    The Art Directors Club
www.fuensanta.com
www.patinunez.com
www.adcglobal.org
Fukunishiki
Tetsuya Hatsusegwa, Issay Kitigawa,
    Juri Tsurumi – Graph
www1.moshi-moshi.jp
www.fukunishiki.co.jp
Fungi Foray Shake O' Cini
Nadia Luciani Howell, Karen Frain,
    Sue Thistlethwaite – L'Acquila
Ken Reilly
www.laquila.co.uk
Gordon's® Gin
Charlotte McCarthy, Sarah Ogilvie –
    Diageo
www.diageo.com
Guinness® Draught
Charlotte McCarthy, Sarah Ogilvie –
    Diageo
www.guinness.com
www.diageo.com

Harvey Nichols Sauce
Anna Davidson, Mary Richards –
    Harvey Nichols
www.harveynichols.com
www.michaelnashassociates.com
'Helvetica'
Danny, Marieke and Erwin –
    Experimental Jetset
www.experimentaljetset.nl
www.plexifilm.com
Hermanos Fernandez
Juan, Rafael and José Hermanos
    Fernández Gonzales
Hermanos Fernandez
Galaroza, Huelva, Spain
Hermès
Fiona Rushton – Hermès
www.hermes.com
IKEA
Charlie Brown, Dawn Smith,
    Helen Squire, Cecilia Cran – IKEA
Peter Samson – PDS Media
www.ikea.com
www.pdsmedia.co.uk
Ines Rosales
Antonio Boza, Juan Espinosa –
    Ines Rosales
Juan Moreno
www.inesrosales.com
Issimbow
Nobue Irako – Nippon Kodo
Shin Matsunaga – Shin
    Matsunaga Design Inc.
www.issimbow.co.jp
www.nipponkodo.com
J&B Rare®
Ewan Topping, Sabine van der Velden,
    Josephine Haining, Sarah Ogilvie –
    Diageo
www.jbscotch.com
www.diageo.com
'The Journal of Popular Noise'
Byron Kalet – Popular Noise
www.popularnoise.net
Kevin Murphy Homme
Kevin Murphy, Janelle Chaplin –
    Kevin Murphy
Mark Shorrock – Reubens Wood
Di Dodding – American Crew UK
Kaniz Abbas – Pure PR
www.kevinmurphystore.com
www.purepr.com
Kiehl's Creme de Corps
Charlotte Adjchavanich – Kiehl's
Claire Nash, Clare Pike – L'Oreal
www.kiehls.com
Kirriemuir Gingerbread
Davina Green, James Maxwell Stuart –
    Bell Bakers
www.bellbakers.co.uk
Klaus 1856 Caramels Tendres
Marianne Mougin – Klaus
www.klaus.com
Korres Aftershave Balm and Lip Butters
Helene Prablanc – Korres
Carly Mason – Chalk PR
www.korres.com
www.k2design.gr
www.chalkpr.co.uk
Kshocolât
Simon Coyle, Andrea Mellon, Amanda
    Treend – Kshocolât
Hector Pottie, Rhona Finlay – Marque
www.kshocolat.co.uk
www.marquecreative.com
Laguiole
Katie Holmes, Carly Morris – Habitat
www.habitat.co.uk
www.jeandubost.com
Leitz Weingut
Michael Neser – Fuenfwerken
www.fuenfwerken.com
www.leitz-wein.de
Levi's® knock-down packs
Kyle Cook – Kyco Creative
www.levistrauss.com
www.driversideimpact.com

Levi's® carrier bags and tissue wrap
Kate Shepherd, Jeff Kindlysides –
    Checkland Kindlysides
www.levistrauss.com
www.checklandkindlysides.com
Liten Ljus Lager
Krönleins Bryggeri
Jörgen Olofsson – Amore
www.kronleins.se
www.amore.se
Magnanni shoe box
Pati Núñez, Esther Martin –
    Pati Núñez Associats
Kimberly Hanzich –
    The Art Directors Club
www.magnanni.com
www.patinunez.com
www.adcglobal.org
Marks & Spencer
Charlotte Raphael, Ann Ledgard –
    Marks & Spencer
www.marksandspencer.com
Maroma Encens d'Auroville
Roma Hira, Laura Reddy, Paul Pinthon –
    Maroma
www.maroma.com
Miss Khoo's Asian Deli
Zerafina Idris – Miss Khoo's Asian Deli
www.misskhoosasiandeli.com
Molton Brown Aircandela
Sarah White – Halpern PR
www.moltonbrown.co.uk
www.halpern.co.uk
Monokuro Boo
Hayashi Hiroaki – San-X Co. Ltd
www.san-x.co.jp
Nikka Whisky
Michael Young, Jess H –
    Michael Young Design
www.nikka.com
www.michael-young.com
Ortiz
Jacobo Múgica, Cécile Bourragué –
    Conservas Ortiz
Claire Roff – Brindisa
www.conservasortiz.com
www.brindisa.com
Orval Trappiste Ale
Augusta Philbiche-Dolsma – Orval
www.orval.be
Paperchase
Dave Howard – Paperchase
Penny Dukes – c/o Paperchase
www.paperchase.co.uk
Paul Smith Extreme
Pauliina Lehtonen, Alan Aboud, Jamie
    Register – Aboud Creative
www.paulsmith.co.uk
www.aboud-creative.com
Paxton & Whitfield
Sara Hall – Paxton & Whitfield
www.paxtonandwhitfield.co.uk
www.royalwarrant.org
Prada
Jessica Pearson, Karim Rashid –
    Karim Rashid
www.prada.com
www.karimrashid.com
Prosays'
Tinky Chan – Tommy Li Design
www.prosays.com
www.tommylidesign.com
Ramune
Yuka Nagano – Japan Sangaria
    Beverage Company
www.sangaria.co.jp
REN
John Perlmutter, Dwayne Lewars – Earth
Vicky Manchett, Jane McNabb –
    Kilpatrick PR
www.renskincare.com
www.earth8.com
www.kilpatrickpr.com
Rosie Fairtrade Tea
Gary McCann, David Craig –
    Espresso Warehouse
www.espressowarehouse.com
www.graven.co.uk

St Peter's Organic Ale
Colin Cordy – St Peter's Brewery
www.stpetersbrewery.co.uk
Saks Fifth Avenue
Kurt Koepfle – Pentagram Design, USA
www.saksfifthavenue.com
www.pentagram.com
Schönberg Ensemble Edition
André Cremer – UNA Designers
www.unadesigners.nl
Scotia Seeds
Giles Laverack, Fiona Guest –
    Scotia Seeds
www.scotiaseeds.co.uk
Scottish Bluebell matches
Anna Lekander, Andrew Wright –
    Swedish Match UK Limited
www.swedishmatch.com
Selfridges & Co
Rosie Buckler, Dave Richmond –
    R Design
www.selfridges.com
www.r-design.co.uk
Selfset Rat Trap
Mike Flint, Lee Towersey – Falcon Works
www.falconworks.co.uk
Shit Happens dog poo bags
Nina Dautzenberg, Andrea Gadesmann –
    Junge Schachtel
www.jungeschachtel.de
www.poopoobags.com
'Signe Quotidiens'
Marco Walser, Valentin Hindermann –
    Elektrosmog
www.esmog.org
Stella In Two
Ben Parker, Paul Austin, Eve Skillicorn –
    MadeThought
www.stellaintwo.com
www.madethought.com
Storm Matches
Carron Tobin, Sharon McLeish –
    Loch Lomond and the Trossachs
    National Park
Jenny Crowe – Galerie Eigen+Art
    Leipzig/Berlin
www.lochlomond-trossachs.org
www.eigen-art.com
Swienty Queen Bee Cage
Bjørn Andresen – Swienty
www.swienty.com
Target ClearRX
Deborah Adler
Denise Mallery – Target
www.target.com
Tesco Ingredients
Wes Anson, Phil Curl –
    Pemberton & Whitefoord
    Design Consultants
www.tesco.com
www.p-and-w.com
Tiffany & Co.
Keith Daigle, Susannah McDonald,
    Jennifer Rittner, Paula Scher,
    Anka Stolman – Pentagram Design, USA
www.tiffany.com
www.pentagram.com
Toblerone
Judi Allan – Kraft Foods
www.kraft.com
www.toblerone.com
Traquair Jacobite Ale
Catherine Maxwell-Stuart –
    Traquair House
Brian Ford/HGV Design
www.traquair.co.uk
www.hgv.co.uk
Trotter Gear
Kirsty Tyrell, Trevor Gulliver –
    St. John Restaurant
www.trottergear.com
Tunnock's
A. Boyd Tunnock
www.tunnocks.co.uk
Ubuntu Cola
Miranda Walker – Ubuntu
Simon Porteous
www.ubuntu-trading.com

'Under the Iron Sea'
Gerard Saint – Big Active
www.bigactive.com
www.keanemusic.com
'The Vanity of Allegory'
Stefan Sagmeister, Joe Shouldice –
    Sagmeister Inc.
www.sagmeister.com
VAT 69®
Nicholas Foot – Diageo
www.diageo.com
Vine Parma
Raya Ivanovskaya
www.ohka.ru
Vintage Stila Eyeshadow
Natasha Hill – Stila Cosmetics
www.stilacosmetics.com
Vitra Eames Plywood Elephant
Birgit Pieles, Joyce Paton –
    Vitra AG, Birsfelden
Genevieve Fo, Roz – Eames
www.vitra.com
www.eamesgallery.com
Vitra now produces the first commercial
production of the legendary Eames Plywood
Elephant as a limited Collector's Edition.
Vitra Design Museum
Charles-Eames-Straße 1
D-79576 Weil am Rhein
Telephone +49 7621 702 32 00
Fax +49 7621 702 31 46
shop@design-museum.com
www.design-museum.com
Voya
Mark Walton – Voya
Wendy Kavanagh – Dynamo
www.dynamo.ie
www.voya.ie
Wallace Land o' Cakes
Alan Fisher, Gwen Fisher –
    Wallace Family Bakers
Wallace Family Bakery
Kingswell, Castle Huntly,
Longforgan, Dundee, Scotland
Winsor and Newton Artists'
Water Colour
Leanne Day – ColArt
www.colart.com
www.winsornewton.com
Wonderwall Brick Tissue Box
Miko Abe – Wonderwall Inc.
Yumiko Iida – Groovisions Inc.
Erin Takagi – Dentsu Inc.
www.nepia.co.jp
www.wonder-wall.com
www.groovisions.com
www.dentsu.com
Woolrich
Andrew Alessandri, Fabio Gamberini –
    D-sign
www.woolrich.com
www.dsign.it
Xocoa
Lydia Bagaria, Marco Escursell – Xocoa
Frank McGarva – Graven Images
www.xocoa-bcn.com
www.mucho.ws
www.graven.co.uk

Index

Picture credits & acknowledgements

Picture credits

The author and publisher would like to thank all individuals, agencies, companies and designers that supplied pictures for use in this book:

p2 photography © Raya Ivanovskaya; p10 courtesy of MadeThought; p12 (1–2) courtesy of Checkland Kindleysides; (3) courtesy of Jungeschachtel; (4) courtesy of Marks & Spencer; (5) © Graven Images; p13 (6) photography by PSc Photography Ltd; (7) © Alexis Taulé; (8) courtesy of Tommy Li Design; (9) courtesy of Hermès; p14 courtesy of Kshocolât; p15–17 photography © Lee Mawdsley; p18–19 courtesy of Kshocolât; p20–21 courtesy of Japan Tobacco International; p22 courtesy of P and W; p23 courtesy of Target; p24 photography © James Shanks; p25 photography © Nick Turner; p26 (1–3) photography © James Shanks/ p26 (4) photography © Nick Turner; p27 photography © Nick Turner /all images courtesy of Tiffany & Co.; p28 photography © Renzo Mazzolini; p29 photography © Josep Gil; p30 photography © Renzo Mazzolini; p31 courtesy of Hermès; p32–37 courtesy of EverEdge IP; p38 courtesy of Kiehl's; p39 photography © Renzo Mazzolini/courtesy of Graven Images; p40–41 photography by PSc Photography Ltd/courtesy of Dr Bronner's; p42 photography by © Renzo Mazzolini; p43 courtesy of Habitat; p44–47 courtesy of Marks & Spencer; p48 photography © Graven Images; p49 courtesy of Stila Corporation; p50–51 courtesy of Tommy Li Design; p52 photography © Renzo Mazzolini; p53 courtesy of Swienty; p54–55 photography by PSc Photography Ltd; p58 courtesy of Karim Rashid; p60 (1) courtesy of Inga Knolke, Image Kontainer; (2) courtesy of Diageo; (3) courtesy of Alexis Taulé; (4) photography © Renzo Mazzolini; p61 (5) photography © Renzo Mazzolini; (6) courtesy of Ortiz; (7) courtesy of Diageo; (8) courtesy of Marks & Spencer; p62–63 © Coe Vintners & Rob Lawson; p64 courtesy of Fee Brothers; p65 © Coe Vintners & Rob Lawson; p66 photography © Graven Images; p67 photography © Renzo Mazzolini; p68 courtesy of Inga Knolke, Image Kontainer; p69 photography © Artur Munoz; p70–73 courtesy of Diageo; p74 courtesy of Ines Rosales; p75 photography by PSc Photography Ltd; p76 courtesy of Klaus; p77 courtesy of Orval; p78–81 courtesy of Ortiz; p82 photography © Stewart Graham, Art Direction: Alan Lorimer; p83 photography © Renzo Mazzolini; p84–85 courtesy of Karim Rashid; p86–89 courtesy of Ubuntu; p90 courtesy of Traquair House; p91 photography © Renzo Mazzolini; p92 photography © Renzo Mazzolini; p93 courtesy of Diageo; p94–95 photography by PSc Photography Ltd; p96 photography by PSc Photography Ltd/ courtesy of St. Peter's Brewery; p97 courtesy of Kraft Foods; p100 courtesy of Marks & Spencer; p102 (1) photography © Alexis Taulé; (2) photography © Renzo Mazzolini; (3) photography © Renzo Mazzolini; (4) photography © Gerrit Burtrock; p103 (5) courtesy Roger Rohr; (6) © Alexis Taulé; (7) courtesy of Comme des Garçons; (8) photography © Graven Images; (9) courtesy of Dylon International Limited; p104–7 courtesy of BP; p108–9 courtesy of Comme des Garçons; p110–11 courtesy of Sagmeister Inc; p112–13 courtesy of Apple; p114–5 photography © Graven Images; p116 photography © Renzo Mazzolini; p117 courtesy of Diageo; p118–19 courtesy of MadeThought; p120 courtesy of Amore; p121 courtesy of Elektrosmog; p122–25 courtesy of Ecopod; p126 photography © Renzo Mazzolini; p127 photography © Renzo Mazzolini with permission from Eames/Three-dimensionally moulded plywood, natural maple, nickle plated screw. 69 x 69 x 130 mm/scale 1:6. After a prototype in the personal collection of Lucia Eames, manufactured and marketed by the Vitra Design Museum, Weil am Rhein/Germany, under the license of the Eames Office (www.eamesoffice.com). All rights reserved.; p128–29 photography © Jan Schultchen; p130 photography by PSc Photography Ltd; p131 photography © Kyle Cook; p132 photography by PSc Photography Ltd; p133–36 photography © Renzo Mazzolini; p136 photography © Atsushi Ueno; p137 courtesy of Molton Brown & Halpern; p138–39 Schonberg Ensemble/courtesy of UNA Designers; p140 photography © Francesco Corlaita; p141 photography by PSc Photography Ltd; p144 courtesy of Michael Young; p146 (1) photography © Apple; (2) courtesy of Mucho; (3) photography © Stavros Papayiannis; (4) © Nick Carmen; p147 (5) courtesy of Michael Young; (6) courtesy of Pentagram USA; (7) photography by PSc Photography Ltd; (8) courtesy of Pentagram UK; (9) courtesy of Graph, Japan; (10) photography © Raya Ivanovskaya; p148–51 courtesy of R Design; p152 © Rodrigo Diaz Wichmann; p153 courtesy of Pentagram; p154–55 photography © Renzo Mazzolini; p156–161 courtesy of Big Active; p162 courtesy of Graph, Japan; p163 photography © Renzo Mazzolini; p164–65 photography © Jeremy Balderson; p166 courtesy of Shin Matsunaga Design Inc.; p167 photography by PSc Photography Ltd; p168–71 courtesy of Wendy Kavanagh & Voya; p172–73 photography by PSc Photography Ltd; p174 photography © Stavros Papayiannis; p175 courtesy of Michael Neser at Fuenfwerken; p176–77 courtesy of Xocoa; p178–79 photography by PSc Photography Ltd; p180 Image © San-X Co., Limited. All rights reserved/ photography © Graven Images; p181 photography © Renzo Mazzolini; p182 courtesy of Pentagram USA ; p183 photography © Nick Carmen; p184 photography © Sandro Sodano/Aboud Creative; p185 photography by PSc Photography Ltd; p186 courtesy of Kolle Rebbe; p187 courtessy of Alessi.

Acknowledgements

Many, many people helped me to write this book. I give my sincere thanks to all who contributed to the project and who took time to talk to me.

To those of you who worked behind the scenes and whose names did not appear in the captions, thank you. Without your help this book would simply not have been possible.

I'd especially like to thank my colleagues at Graven Images, particularly Emma Murphy for her painstaking research, reasonably good humour and colourful language, Ross Hunter for his endless criticism (some of which I agreed with), Tony Blow, Colin Chau, Nik Herbert and Joanna Martin for their helpful suggestions and Helen McGarvey and Andrew Sutherland for their superlative Excel spreadsheets. And Frank McGarva who shopped for chocolate in Barcelona then ate the lot.

I wouldn't have got far without support from my excellent agent Barbara Levy, who's sound judgement, encouragement and serenity throughout the project inspired me and illuminated the road ahead.

For contributions beyond the call of duty I'd also like to give thanks to Jony Ive for making it possible for me to include Apple's fabulous packaging, Jan Nimmo and Chaparro in beautiful Andalucia for help with Spanish translation and research, Jeremy Sutton-Hibbert for kindly photographing packs in Tokyo, Ayumi Sakurazawa for her Japanese translations, Catherine Docherty at Journey Associates for supporting Japanese contributors, David Kester at the Design Council for his encouragement and help with research, Renzo Mazzolini for graciously agreeing to photograph packs rather than people, Joyce Paton at Vitra in Glasgow for support regarding Eames' plywood elephant pack, Lucy Pritchard, Josephine Haining and Ewan Topping at Diageo for allowing me to visit their amazing archive, Dorenda Brittain from designindustry for introducing me to Crushpak, Lucy Byatt from The Centre for explaining the story behind Storm Matches, Tanja Gertick from Art Management for help with research and Nick Barley, Julia Fenby, Leonie Bell and Lucy McEachan at The Lighthouse for support and help with research. Last, but not least, thanks to Daniel Ibbotson at GraphicalHouse and Helen Evans, Zoe Antoniou and Laurence King Publishing for inviting me to write the book in the first place and for trusting me to get the job done.

Janice Kirkpatrick, *Graven Images*